CHILDREN OF MANZANAR

Photo by Toyo Miyatake, courtesy of Toyo Miyatake Studio

CHILDREN OF MANZANAR

Edited by Heather C. Lindquist

Foreword by Mary Daniel

Epilogue by Alisa Lynch

Heyday, Berkeley, California · Manzanar History Association, Independence, California

Library of Congress Cataloging-in-Publication Data

Children of Manzanar / edited by Heather C. Lindquist ; foreword by Mary Daniel ; epilogue by Alisa Lynch.
    p. cm.
Includes bibliographical references.
ISBN 978-1-59714-160-4 (pbk. : alk. paper)
 1. Japanese American children--California--Manzanar--History--20th century. 2. Manzanar War Relocation Center--History. 3. Children--California--Manzanar--History--20th century. 4. Japanese Americans--Interviews. 5. Japanese Americans--Evacuation and relocation, 1942-1945. 6. Japanese American children--California--Manzanar--History--20th century--Pictorial works. 7. Manzanar War Relocation Center--History--Pictorial works. 8. Children--California--Manzanar--History--20th century--Pictorial works. I. Lindquist, Heather C.
D769.8.A6C37 2012
940.53'1779487--dc23
          2011046404

Cover photo by Katsumi Taniguchi, courtesy of Manzanar National Historic Site
Book design by Lorraine Rath

Orders, inquiries, and correspondence should be addressed to:
    Heyday
    P.O. Box 9145, Berkeley, CA 94709
    (510) 549-3564, Fax (510) 549-1889
    www.heydaybooks.com

Printed in China by Everbest Printing Co. through Four Colour Imports, Ltd., Louisville, Kentucky

10 9 8 7 6 5 4 3 2

There is only one place called Manzanar, California. Yet there is no single, simple story about it.

This book is dedicated to the children of Manzanar.
For each, there is a different story about growing up "behind those wires."

Boy with toy gun.

Photo from the Hosoi family, courtesy of Manzanar National Historic Site

CONTENTS

Teenage girls approach the lunch line at one of Manzanar's thirty-six mess halls, 1943.

FOREWORD

It was a profoundly moving experience to walk into the nearly complete interpretive center at Manzanar National Historic Site a few months prior to opening day, in April 2004. In the hushed, expansive exhibit hall—once the school gymnasium for Japanese American teenagers interned at the camp—I felt the presence of the more than 10,000 people whose lives had been irreversibly altered in this place. Everywhere I looked, enlarged photographs of the individuals who once lived at Manzanar bore witness to their unwelcome challenges. These people lived behind barbed wire fences—uprooted from their homes, their businesses gone, and their prospects bleak. This was clearly an anxious, frightening, and sad interlude. But as my work continued and the years unfolded, it was the photos of the children that made me pause again and again, and if photographs convey truths, as I believe they do, we see in the images of these young people—remarkably—evidence of that joyous abandon unique to childhood. Under the eyes of armed guards, babies laughed, children lost themselves in marble and baseball games alike, and teenagers danced the foxtrot. However different we are from one another now, no doubt our early years were infused with a spirit and energy common to children everywhere, and this was true even for children in camp.

As you move slowly through the following pages, you'll witness this range of emotion—from sadness to joy—and perhaps marvel at the moments of profound resilience in the face of the most egregious wartime policies. It's complicated, I know, but these perspectives of the children of Manzanar might surprise you.

Mary Daniel
Manzanar History Association

In growing up, especially during the camp experience, we were put in a situation where all our neighbors were just like us: black hair and brown eyes. I think I had a more difficult time in junior high and high school, and even into my early adult years, of making friends with Caucasians. I don't know if that camp experience kind of taught me to be more guarded, or maybe I was just more comfortable with Japanese friends....We lived together for three years with people of our own makeup. Maybe I just feel more comfortable that way.

—Arthur Yamada, age 8 when he arrived at Manzanar

A third-grader practices freehand drawing, February 1943.

Photo by Francis Stewart, courtesy of the National Archives and Records Administration

Ready to play ball, July 1942.

Photo by Dorothea Lange, courtesy of the National Archives and Records Administration

Louise Tami Nakamura.

Photo by Ansel Adams, courtesy of the Library of Congress

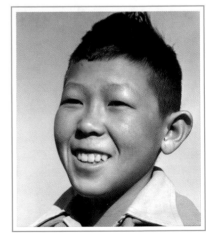

Katsumi Yoshimura.

Photo by Ansel Adams, courtesy of the Library of Congress

Memorial Day, May 1942.

Photo by Francis Stewart, courtesy of the National Archives and Records Administration

Madelon Arai Yamamoto.

Photo from the Yamamoto family, courtesy of Manzanar National Historic Site

Joyce Yuki Nakamura.

Photo by Ansel Adams, courtesy of the Library of Congress

This has become a kind of blank spot in our memory. It has become a blank spot because what happened to us, as a generation, was that as children we were always told to be proud that we were Japanese, but what they did to us in this place...they made us feel ashamed of being Japanese. And for that reason many people just don't talk about it.

—Mas Okui, age 10 when he arrived at Manzanar

Janet Fujino Kishiyama.

Photo by Dorothea Lange, courtesy of the National Archives and Records Administration

Memorial Day, May 1942.

Photo by Francis Stewart, courtesy of the National Archives and Records Administration

AMERICAN BIRTHRIGHTS, JAPANESE BLOODLINES

From 1942 to 1945, more than 3,700 infants, toddlers, children, and teens called Manzanar "home." They grew up during a national crisis. The civil liberties that should have been their birthright as American citizens were denied them during wartime. Their bloodlines marked them to be segregated from their non-Japanese peers and playmates. They left their homes, friends, and pets behind. High school students missed senior proms, college students shelved their studies, couples rushed or postponed wedding plans, and everyone set aside their dreams.

Decades after they left camp, many gave voice to their memories of Manzanar, in oral histories, public testimonies, and memoirs. Echoes of some of these voices ring out on the following pages.

LEAVING HOME AND ARRIVING AT MANZANAR

During the decades leading up to World War II, most of the nearly 127,000 Japanese and Japanese Americans living in the continental United States lived along the West Coast. Many first-generation immigrants (*Issei*) worked as truck farmers, fishermen, merchants, and white-collar workers in typically segregated neighborhoods and business districts, many with the hopes that their children and grandchildren (*Nisei* and *Sansei*, respectively) would attend college, earn professional degrees, and enjoy the full measure of their American citizenship. These later generations—Americans by birth, Japanese by heritage—often embraced two cultures at once. At her public school in Seattle, Monica Sone remembers being "a jumping, screaming, roustabout Yankee," but at Japanese-language school, where the culture and expectations were different, she "suddenly became a modest, faltering, earnest little Japanese girl with a small, timid voice."

PEARL HARBOR AND EO 9066

For Monica and other Japanese American children growing up around 1941, Japan's attack on the U.S. naval base at Pearl Harbor, Hawaii, changed everything, almost overnight. "The whole world turned dark," Mary Tsukamoto says of December 7, 1941. The U.S. Congress declared war on Japan the next day, and on Germany and Italy three days after that. Two months later, on February 19, 1942, President Franklin D. Roosevelt signed Executive Order 9066 (EO 9066), authorizing the U.S. military to carry out the exclusion and detention of American citizens and resident aliens for purposes of national security. Although the order did not specify any ethnic group by name, in practice it applied to some German and Italian aliens as individuals and to *all* people of Japanese ancestry living on the West Coast.

For residents of Terminal Island in California's San Pedro Harbor—then a commercial fishing village—daily life had already changed drastically, weeks before EO 9066 went into effect. Immediately following Japan's attack, the U.S. Federal Bureau of Investigation rounded up all Japanese American community leaders and took fishermen returning from the sea into immediate custody. Teenagers who usually rode the ferry to school were sent back home. Blocked from fishing, and with funds in Japanese branch banks frozen, families lost their livelihoods instantaneously. Ten days after the signing of EO 9066, the U.S. Navy took control of Terminal Island, ordering residents to leave their homes within forty-eight hours. More than three thousand islanders had to find temporary shelter and endure weeks of uncertainty before they were ultimately sent to Manzanar and other "assembly centers" in April of 1942. (It's important to note that the term "assembly center," like many others used to refer to forced removal and confinement during and after the war, is a euphemism; for clarification, see the Terminology section beginning on page 133.) At Manzanar many of the Terminal Islander teens—often considered very "Japanesey" by others—later formed gangs, gaining a reputation as toughs and thugs.

At the same time in the Pacific Northwest, residents of another island community—one similarly strategic to U.S. military interests—became the first to face immediate removal under EO 9066. During the last six days of March 1942, the U.S. Army rounded up all members of the relatively small Japanese American community on Bainbridge Island and sent them south to Manzanar. As Ichiro Nagatani described his community's dilemma at the time, "We are just as good Americans as the next guy, only we haven't had a chance to prove it."

As the army issued similar orders up and down the West Coast, all people of Japanese ancestry attempted to prepare for an uncertain future. Many sold property at steep losses, gave away pets, and burned or buried photographs, letters, and heirlooms from Japan. Most had less than two weeks to pack "only what they could carry."

ARRIVING AT MANZANAR

Throughout the spring of 1942 the U.S. Army mobilized rapidly to carry out the mass forced removal. Taking over racetracks, fairgrounds, and parks, it hastily prepared seventeen temporary facilities, including the Owens Valley Reception Center, which later became Manzanar War Relocation Center. Buses, trains, and convoys of cars delivered hundreds of new arrivals each day. Years after Grace Shinoda Nakamura arrived at Manzanar on May 16, 1942, she could still "remember vividly the plight of the elderly, some on stretchers, orphans herded onto the train by caretakers, and especially a young couple with four preschool children. The mother had two frightened toddlers hanging on to her coat. In her arms, she carried two crying babies. The father had diapers and other baby paraphernalia strapped to his back. In his hands he struggled with a duffle bag and suitcase."

Under duress and in a climate of profound uncertainty, internees tried to adjust to life in the assembly centers, not knowing how long they would be held there, or where they would be sent next. Children attended classes, families created makeshift homes, and many adults worked as cooks, mess hall staff, police clerks, teachers, nurses, and doctors. Within months, though, most Japanese and Japanese Americans were moved yet again, to more permanent War Relocation Centers. The U.S. government constructed these ten camps on public lands in remote deserts, plains, and swamps. Populations of the camps ranged from 7,318 at Amache to 18,789 at Tule Lake. During the course of the war, 11,070 Japanese Americans were confined at Manzanar. Two-thirds were *Nisei*, American citizens by birth. Nearly 4,000 were under eighteen years of age prior to their arrival. "When we first got here," Dorothy Sugihara remembers, "I saw the [guard] tower; that scared me to death 'cause we're not used to seeing that and the barbed wire. That made it [feel] like you are in there for good."

THE WAR RELOCATION AUTHORITY

In late spring of 1942 the War Relocation Authority (WRA) took over for the Wartime Civil Control Administration (WCCA), which had previously run the assembly centers. The civilian-run WRA assumed control of Manzanar on June 1, 1942, with a skeleton staff and the daunting responsibility to care for the basic needs of more than 10,000 people, which included providing shelter, food, healthcare, and a clothing allowance. Recruiting employees proved difficult; wartime defense work offered better pay, less isolation, and did not require living and working with "the Japanese." However, more than two hundred staff members eventually came to work at Manzanar as administrators, teachers, social workers, clerks, engineers, and supervisors, and in a variety of other positions. A number of WRA administrators had worked previously with displaced populations, some with the Office of Indian Affairs or California's migrant worker populations.

At Manzanar, most WRA staff eventually lived in the separate Administration Area, which had its own housing and mess and recreation halls. Some internees called the residential area Beverly Hills, for its indoor plumbing, kitchens, and air conditioning. Erica Harth, the daughter of a WRA worker, remembers, "The administrative section where we lived was literally white. Its white painted bungalows stared across at the rows of brown tarpaper barracks that housed the internees."

Wearing tags identifying their family by number, parents and children wait to board the train from Los Angeles to the Owens Valley.

Photo by Russell Lee, courtesy of the Library of Congress

I remember rumors going through. They said we were going to a very desolate, desert place. We didn't know where we're going, but there was going to be scorpions *this* big and snakes and mosquitoes....I felt particularly sad about leaving my home,...leaving some of my favorite things that I couldn't take with me, and then, of course, my Caucasian friends, I hated to leave.

—Rose Honda, age 15 when she arrived at Manzanar

Somewhere along the way, either before we got to camp or when we arrived, I heard some people talking and someone said that we would be in camp the rest of our lives. I believed it.

—Victor Muraoka, age 9 when he arrived at Manzanar

Men, women, and children board a bus in Lone Pine, California, on April 1, 1942, for the last leg of their journey to Manzanar.

Photo by Clem Albers, courtesy of the National Archives and Records Administration

Bound for Manzanar, Bainbridge Islander Fumiko Hayashida cradles her sleeping daughter, Natalie, March 30, 1942.

Photo from the Post-Intelligencer Collection, courtesy of the Museum of History and Industry, Seattle, Washington

During the Bainbridge Island removal process, a soldier holds Jane Nakamura on the way to the ferry terminal, March 30, 1942.

Photo from the Post-Intelligencer Collection, courtesy of the Museum of History and Industry, Seattle, Washington

Photo by Russell Lee, courtesy of the Library of Congress

I remember that our mom bought us good clothes and feathered hats. I don't know why we dressed that way, since we were headed to camp, but in those days I really didn't understand the enormity of what was happening.

—Victor Muraoka

Following instructions to pack "only what they could carry," two-year-old Keith Miyamoto and his family leave San Francisco on April 6, 1942.

International News Photo, University of Southern California Library, Department of Special Collections, Regional History Collection

Flanked by news photographers, two boys leave their Van Ness Avenue neighborhood in San Francisco, April 6, 1942.

Photo by Dorothea Lange, courtesy of the National Archives and Records Administration

We heard the news on the radio and naturally we thought it was a very terrible thing. I kind of felt ashamed because we were Japanese, and Japan would have the audacity to invade American soil. A lot of my classmates were afraid to go to school the following Monday for fear of reprisals, but I didn't feel that way. I really didn't feel Japanese, if that makes any sense, because the only connection I had was that my [ethnicity] was Japanese.

—Sam Ono, age 15 when he arrived at Manzanar

The pain came, at that time, not from what officials said but from California teachers: "Do you think your army will invade us?" Merchants refusing to serve us. Leaving for Manzanar, acquaintances saying, "It's for your own protection." Loonies waving fists and cursing at us as the buses departed for Manzanar.

—Sohei Hohri, age 17 when he arrived at Manzanar

A San Francisco store owner shutters his store in response to EO 9066.

Courtesy of the Library of Congress

"Evacuation sale" in Florin, California, May 11, 1942.

Photo by Dorothea Lange, courtesy of the National Archives and Records Administration

A few families had trusted neighbors who took care of their farms and property for the duration of the war. Most, however, lost their leases and sold possessions at steep losses. Here, the Nakamura family leaves its Bainbridge Island home and farm, March 30, 1942.

Photo from the Post-Intelligencer Collection, courtesy of the Museum of History and Industry, Seattle, Washington

Below: Arriving at Lone Pine, California, May 1, 1942.

Photo by Clem Albers, courtesy of The Bancroft Library, University of California, Berkeley (Negative: 1967.014 v. 19 CA-304—PIC)

At the time, at twelve years old, you might call it an adventure. You are going somewhere where you haven't been before. You don't know what's there and so it was kind of a surprise adventure, [even though we were] scared and had kind of mixed emotions.

—Nob Kamibayashi, age 12 when he arrived at Manzanar

The forced removal happened in stages by truck (such as this one leaving from San Pedro, California), train, bus, and even personal automobile.

Photo by Clem Albers, courtesy of the National Archives and Records Administration

I think the most difficult things to leave behind were memorabilia of family. We did have a few pictures. We didn't take them to camp with us because we didn't know what was going to happen....Apparently there were some unscrupulous people that backed a van [up to the community center where we stored our things], and they just loaded the van up and took off. The neighbors around the community center never thought anything about it because people were always having their friends pick up different things from the so-called warehouse and bringing it up to camp when they were allowed to. Well, when these people came and they just loaded the van and took whatever they wanted away, it happened to be some of our stuff. Everything of my childhood memory went with them. It was no value to them, so I presume it's probably buried in some dumpsite now. —Sam Ono

I was more excited because we were going somewhere else. We're not going to stay here anymore, we're going somewhere else. We got on a bus, then we got on a train. You're still a young person so it's kind of a big deal—not knowing that you were really getting kicked out of San Francisco at that time. When we got into Manzanar, there were more orphanage kids from different areas, so we had to get to know them; it's another family you're getting together with....We knew we were going to another orphanage, that's all.

—Tamotsu Isozaki, age 15 when he arrived at Manzanar's Children's Village

Photo by Clem Albers, courtesy of the National Archives and Records Administration

Under armed guard, with window shades drawn, trains shuttle Japanese Americans as far as Lone Pine, California, where they next board buses for Manzanar, ten miles north, April 1, 1942.

Photo by Clem Albers, courtesy of the National Archives and Records Administration

One of the things I remember on that bus was that there was a little boy younger than I was....As soon as he got on that bus and that bus started moving he had to go to the bathroom and his mother was very, very worried and didn't know what to do. All of a sudden someone produced a soda pop bottle and said, "Here you are!" That did the trick. —Nob Kamibayashi

Photo by Clem Albers, courtesy of The Bancroft Library, University of California, Berkeley (Negative: 1967.014 v. 56 GA-240-PIC)

Photo by Clem Albers, courtesy of The Bancroft Library, University of California, Berkeley (Negative: 1967.014 v. 19 CA-296-PIC)

I remember a very long ride, and I probably slept most of the time because at that period of my life I used to get carsick....When we arrived at Manzanar, it was dusk, and it was cold. And first thing when we got off, they gave us...some kind of shot. Typhoid shot.

—Rose Honda

A Japanese American nurse assists a young family upon arrival at Manzanar, May 1, 1942.

Photo by Clem Albers, courtesy of the National Archives and Records Administration

Camp staff and internee medical professionals vaccinate children against pertussis, diphtheria, tetanus, and typhoid.

Photo from Jack and Peggy Iwata, courtesy of the Japanese American National Museum (93.102.39)

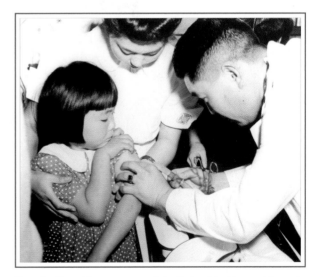

Photo by Clem Albers, courtesy of the National Archives and Records Administration

Photo from Jack and Peggy Iwata, courtesy of the Japanese American National Museum (93.102.180)

I remember seeing military police there, and as we came through the camp up this road, it seems like there was just a wall of people on both sides as we came by. They were silent and as we looked at them they looked forlorn and desolate and hopeless. And we just came in and we kept moving and suddenly the bus stopped, the guards were there, and we got off and no one said anything. We were almost in shocked disbelief.

—Mas Okui, age 10 when he arrived at Manzanar

Removed from their homes in San Pedro, California, Japanese Americans disembark at Santa Anita Assembly Center, a converted racetrack.
Courtesy of the National Archives and Records Administration

Hundreds of Japanese Americans arrive daily, sometimes late into the night. They receive barracks assignments, mattress ticking to stuff with straw, army cots, and blankets.
Photo by Clem Albers, courtesy of the National Archives and Records Administration

I had envisioned Manzanar as a camp of little white cottages for each family, like the ones at Sequoia National Park where we had stayed during vacations. I can still vividly recall my dismay as we pulled into Manzanar… and saw rows of black tarpapered barracks, some…still being built.

—Momo Nagano, age 16 when she arrived at Manzanar

Boys gaze at one of Manzanar's eight guard towers, visible in the middle distance, 1943.

Photo by Katsumi Taniguchi, courtesy of Manzanar National Historic Site

I did not at first think too much about what had happened to the Japanese. To me, it was just how things were. We didn't talk about it very much. I was told they were in the camp because some might be traitors, and we had no way of telling who they might be. Some time later, after reading *Betrayal from the East,* I understood why our government had been so scared of them. To me, the worst part of what happened was that so many had their property taken from them.

—Joan DaValle Beyers, age 12 when she arrived at Manzanar, where her mother, Marjorie G. Mount, taught high school math

Nearly two hundred War Relocation Authority staff members worked as teachers, administrators, counselors, and clerks at Manzanar. They and their children lived in the section known as the Administration Area. Junior high and high school children attended school in Independence, a town six miles north of camp. Elementary school children attended classes inside camp alongside Japanese American students. Joan (*left*) and Shirley DaValle outside the barracks they initially lived in, alongside Japanese American families.

Courtesy of Joan and Shirley DaValle

Children of WRA staff gather in the administration housing area: *(back row, left to right)* George Abel, Shirley DaValle, and Joan DaValle; *(front row, left to right)* Tom Williams, Norma Strong, LaPriel Strong, and Ann Causey, May 1944.
Courtesy of Joan and Shirley DaValle

We lived inside the fence, with nothing to separate us from the Japanese, but did not often mingle. I felt comfortable in my little part of camp, but not in theirs. It was like there was a force field separating us. It was not there to see, but it could be felt.

—Art Williams, age 14 when he arrived at Manzanar, where his father worked as Assistant Chief of Internal Security

Children of WRA staff members.

Photo from Lois Yuki, courtesy of Manzanar National Historic Site

On a few occasions, some Japanese American boys came down to play football on the grass next to our staff mess hall. One time, we went up and played tackle without protective equipment on the dirt firebreak, and there was a lot of hide peeled off. The word got out, and hundreds of people came to watch the game.

—Art Williams

NO MORE FAMILY FEELING

CHILDHOOD IN CONFINEMENT

Family life continued under drastically altered conditions in camp. Room assignments kept families together but often required them to live with strangers in order to achieve the typical total of eight people per room. Privacy was scarce. Rosie Maruki Kakuuchi, a teenager at Manzanar, found using the latrines and showers with no partitions particularly "embarrassing, humiliating, and degrading." In many cases, communal living weakened family ties and undermined parental authority. "As children we all ate separately with our friends," remembers Chiyeko "Chickie" Hiraoka Matoba. "My older brother worked in the mess hall. My younger brother worked as a dishwasher someplace, so our family never ate together. That was a sad, sad thing about that."

At Manzanar, people ate cafeteria-style. Children and teens ganged together, and their parents fed toddlers at separate mealtimes. Some adults feared that, with less parental supervision, children would be "little savages" by the time they left camp. "My mother couldn't control me," Ted Ikeda recalls. "I could eat wherever I wanted to; I didn't eat with her."

In 1944, Dr. Genevieve W. Carter, the superintendent of education at Manzanar, described daily life for many of her students: "Children have not seen a kitchen stove, a bathtub, a family dinner table, or the privacy of a backyard for two years....Their poems, stories, and pictures reflect a barren world of watchtowers, barbed wire fence, tarpapered barracks, desert flora, and high mountains capped with snow." While growing up in this "barren world," though, the children of Manzanar variously played, fought, and studied, just like children everywhere. They sneaked past the barbed wire to go fishing, played marbles in the dust, and formed lifelong friendships. They also saw their parents become powerless, witnessed systemic injustice, and faced an uncertain future. No two stories are the same, yet they share a common thread: young people experienced Manzanar very differently than their parents and grandparents did.

Family life for many people changed suddenly and often permanently in camp. Some fathers and a few mothers were detained in separate U.S. Department of Justice camps, often under unspecified charges and for unspecified periods of time. Even when reunited with their families in camps, some struggled to resume their roles as heads of household, especially since bare essentials like housing, food, and clothing were provided by the War Relocation Authority. Once respected patriarchs, many Japanese and Japanese American men saw their roles as providers and authority figures usurped by the government, camp administrators, and WRA rules and regulations. Quite simply, for Chiyeko "Chickie" Hiraoka Matoba, "It ruined the family structure. Parents were no longer in charge of their children...; there was no more family feeling anymore."

As some young people saw it, grownups who previously had shunned all luxuries and worked long days outside of camp suddenly had too little purpose and too much leisure time. "With older people, there was always a lack of something to do," Mas Okui says. Some took adult education classes (generally English as a foreign language, American history, or citizenship), produced arts and crafts, and worked. Others played *go*, gossiped, and gambled. Many children, meanwhile, ran free—within Manzanar's confines. Decades later, Ted Ikeda reflects: "Yeah, I was in prison, but I didn't feel that I was in prison. It's coming from someone that was in their early teens. Hey, I could do whatever I wanted to do. I wasn't a troublemaker or anything like that, and we never got in fights, and we didn't steal or anything like that. And everything was safe. We just played."

EDUCATION

For the first three months of its operation, Manzanar offered children no formal schooling. It housed 2,300 relocated students, yet there were no classrooms, textbooks, or teachers. In June 1942 the Education Department "started in the corner of one barrack," reported the *Manzanar Free Press*, the internee-run, WRA-censored camp newspaper, similar to others at all ten camps. A ninth-grader at the time, Yuri

Yamazaki Matsunaga recalls "sitting on the floor in a bare room without any desks or chairs." It took a few months for the school to receive used textbooks from the Los Angeles Unified School District and other sources, but classrooms remained under-equipped, particularly those for science labs. In eighth grade, Mas Okui's science classroom was "simply a barrack room. And what they had done is taken a piece of plywood and painted it black, and that was our blackboard. And we sat there on these long [benches] with no backrests, and I can remember the teacher, he was a Japanese American teacher...; anytime he talked about science, he would say, 'Pretend that this is a Bunsen burner,' or whatever it is, and after a while the kids in the class would simply pretend."

Within a year, however, the *Manzanar Free Press* reported that "about 50 percent of the total community population is going to school." The elementary school enrolled 1,300 students, the secondary school 1,400, and the adult education program 2,050. The WRA initiated an "Americanization" program in May 1942, with adult English language, democracy, and U.S. history classes taught by internees. By the time Yuri Yamazaki Matsunaga graduated from Manzanar High School in 1945, an accredited staff was teaching a standard curriculum in the barracks classrooms.

Most of the teaching staff was Caucasian. A few, like choir director Louis Frizzell and journalism teacher Janet Goldberg, became quite beloved. Local superintendent Dorothy Cragen "used to wonder how the children could get up and sing such patriotic songs. They would sing, 'I am an American' and all the songs we sang in our [regular public] schools."

Over time, through sports and other extracurricular activities, Manzanar students were able to meet members of their cohort from Owens Valley schools outside camp. The Manzanar school paper, *Campus Pepper,* optimistically tracked Principal Rollin Fox's invitations to "neighboring high schools asking for games with Manzanar Hi." In October 1944, one student journalist wrote, "Let us all hope that the answer will be 'YES.'"

SCHOOL SPORTS

On at least one notable occasion, a "yes" for an away game for the boys' basketball team turned into a "no." As recorded in a WRA report, "A few hours before the Manzanar boys were to leave for Bishop, and after the proper clearance with the Western Defense Command had been effected, the Bishop high school board canceled the game, explaining that they were concerned lest there be some community protest over it. The president of the Bishop student body sent a letter to the Manzanar high school explaining the position of its students. Because of its interest in showing the attitude of the young people as opposed to that of their more intolerant parents, a copy of the letter is included in this report":

BISHOP, CALIFORNIA
January 23, 1945

Student Body
Manzanar Secondary School
Manzanar, California

Dear Students:
We were glad to receive the understanding letter sent us by your principal, Mr. Rollin Fox.

When we were informed that the game with your basketball team had been canceled we did our utmost to change the School Board's decision through a petition signed by the entire student body. It has been taught us in school that a democracy and constitution such as ours guarantees every American equal treatment. Certain members of the Board, however, refused to acknowledge our efforts.

We sincerely hope arrangements can be made for another game with your team.

Sincerely yours,
Mickey Duffy (Signed)
Student Body President

Manzanar students, in fact, never left camp to compete against students in other Owens Valley schools. Big Pine was the only school ever to come to Manzanar to compete in sports—and only once at that. Almost all social events between Owens Valley and Manzanar youth took place inside the camp's confines. Kerry Christenson Powell, a young Camp Fire Girl from a nearby town, never forgot her afternoon with members of Manzanar's Girl Scout troop. "To me it was only exciting to get to go into the guarded gate and actually see the place about which we were naturally curious. We met the attractive, neat, and friendly Girl Scouts at a beautiful, small, bright green grass park that was created in what I realized was a typical spare Japanese style. We were all in our simple uniforms. I felt immature, as they were a bit older group. The main difference was that they all had dark brown/black straight hair." The afternoon exchange included invitations to visit individual troop members' barracks apartments. "What I remember most was a simple, small dresser, as for a bedroom, beside the front door with a framed photo of the girl's Japanese brother in an American army uniform. She explained to me that he was serving in the war in Europe. Seeing that picture made me very sad, and it all seemed so unfair that she had to be living like that in there."

At times, exchanges between kids inside Manzanar and the outside world happened more anonymously and over much longer distances. On Mas Okui's first Christmas in camp, his family had no extra money for gifts, but he still received a present through a church donation program: "Of all the Christmases in my sixty-nine years, this is the only gift I remember," he recalled in 1993.

Many young people saw snow for the first time at Manzanar. George Shimatsu described the moment for his elementary school paper, the *Manzanar Whirlwind:* "The house, tree, and the ground was white with it. I ran out and got some snow to throw at Billy, but he threw snowballs at me before I was ready. We had lots of fun."

With more than eighty organized baseball teams in the camp, and thousands of impromptu games taking place in the firebreaks between barracks blocks, America's favorite pastime had enormous significance at Manzanar. To a lesser degree, so did *judo, kendo,* and other sports. Mirroring the bicultural nature of life in Manzanar, children's activities expressed both their Japanese heritage—Buddhism, martial arts, and traditional festivals—and typical hallmarks of American culture—cheerleading, big band music, and football. "We imported much of America into the camps because, after all, we were Americans," John Tateishi reflects. "I was learning, as best one could learn in Manzanar, what it meant to live in America. But I was also learning the sometimes bitter price one has to pay for it."

We were told that we would live in this barrack, this twenty-five-foot barrack room. We looked at it and we were told that in Block 17, this is where we would live. We walked in there and it had wood on the floor and there were spaces between the wood. You could see the dirt underneath. And they had one naked lightbulb hanging down and they had army cots. They had eight army cots there. I can remember what they gave us was a couple of blankets, a big canvas bag, and I looked at the army cots and they looked funny because they were high and had, apparently, been hospital cots. Then we were told that we would fill the canvas bags with straw and they would be our mattresses. And it was just the four of us—my father, two brothers, and myself—in this 20'x25' room. And all of a sudden another family of four came into this same room.

—Mas Okui, age 10 when he arrived at Manzanar

Cloth partitions provide scant privacy for families assigned to share a single 20'x25' barracks apartment, June 1942.
Photo by Dorothea Lange, courtesy of the National Archives and Records Administration

Mealtime in a mess hall, July 1942.

Photo by Dorothea Lange, courtesy of the National Archives and Records Administration

Our first meal was in our mess hall, where we picked up army mess kits (the same kind I would use later in Korea) and got in line with the rest of the inmates. We had family with us, including the Hamamoto clan, the Muraokas, and other relatives, along with other farmers from the North Hollywood area. Eating in a mess hall with familiar faces made it easier to take. I don't recall what we ate the first day, but many of us were getting used to the mess kits, and I noticed I was not the only one who spilled his drink because I did not properly fix the metal mess cup.

—Victor Muraoka, age 9 when he arrived at Manzanar

The Uchida family, friends, and neighbors gather in Florin, California, 1916.

Photo from the Japanese American Archival Collection, Department of Special Collections and University Archives, The Library, California State University, Sacramento

Decades later, three generations of the Uchida family assemble for a group portrait at Manzanar.

Photo from the Japanese American Archival Collection, Department of Special Collections and University Archives, The Library, California State University, Sacramento

This "Manzanar Mansion" sign identifies three families—Kubota, Miya, and Shindo—sharing the same barracks. As barracks construction nears completion in summer 1942, overcrowding lessens.

Photo by Clem Albers, courtesy of the National Archives and Records Administration

Third-graders, 1943.

Photo by Ansel Adams, courtesy of the Library of Congress

Actually, we didn't have what you would call a "family life." We were in the same apartment, but I would go to school, come back; I would go to the music hall, practice, or the library. My mother worked at the mess hall, my father was a Manzanar carpenter, and my sister was a librarian at the school library. Midori was an elementary school teacher....So the family life was not together, although we lived in the apartment together. We weren't going as a group anywhere; we all had separate lives.

—Bruce Kaji, age 17 when he arrived at Manzanar

Memorial Day, May 1942.

Photo by Francis Stewart, courtesy of the National Archives and Records Administration

I think parental control became fairly lax because in camp where could you go? They knew that you were in the confines of camp, and if you were in Block 35, the farthest you could be is Block 12. So parents didn't really worry about where their children were. I think that, to me, was one of the tragedies of being interned.

—Sam Ono, age 15 when he arrived at Manzanar

Preschoolers leave a typical barracks classroom, July 1, 1942.

Photo by Dorothea Lange, courtesy of the National Archives and Records Administration

Ken and Kay Utsunomiya, 1943.
Photo from the Hosoi family, courtesy of Manzanar National Historic Site

Below: Mr. Tanabe and neighbor children at Manzanar.
Photo by Katsumi Taniguchi, courtesy of Manzanar National Historic Site

My father used to always talk to us. He would sit us down in the evening and, in a sense, he would talk about the philosophy of life, which we didn't understand as little children. But when we came to this camp, the only time we saw our father was when we went back to the apartment to sleep, 'cause we stayed outside most of the time....If there was a disintegration of the Japanese family, which has always been one of the strong points of our subculture, it probably occurred here.

—Mas Okui

First steps, July 3, 1942.

Photo by Dorothea Lange, courtesy of the National
Archives and Records Administration

My father was taken in by the FBI on Monday, December 8, and from there traveled from one alien enemy detention camp to another....Later on my father was released from Santa Fe to come back to us at Manzanar....It was a break to have my father back because I hadn't seen him. At that age not seeing your father for a couple of years is quite a long time.

—Nob Kamibayashi, age 12 when he arrived at Manzanar

The Arai family in front of barracks, 1943.

Photo from the Hosoi family, courtesy of Manzanar National Historic Site

I can remember my mother taking baths or showers at two o'clock in the afternoon [because the stalls wouldn't be crowded then]....It was this true lack of privacy that we were forced to live in that made things difficult for the women.

—Mas Okui

Photo from the Hosoi family, courtesy of Manzanar National Historic Site

I guess it was, in one sense, kind of a stressful thing for my mother and father, probably, having to raise children in that kind of environment.

—Arthur Yamada, age 8 when he arrived at Manzanar

In the yard between barracks, 1943.

Photos from the Hirosawa family, courtesy of Manzanar National Historic Site

When we first went into camp, in early 1942, there was no organized education. We played from early morning to late at night.

—Nob Kamibayashi

Impromptu baseball games take place almost every day. Soon after their arrival, these boys start to play ball, April 2, 1942.
Photo by Clem Albers, courtesy of the National Archives and Records Administration

I can remember the dust storms that we had at camp, and these winds that whirl around, and the kids would jump right in the middle of them. Oh, they thought it was such fun.

—Taeko Kajiwara Nagayama, age 21 when she arrived to work at Manzanar's Children's Village

Photo by Toyo Miyatake, courtesy of Toyo Miyatake Studio

Richard and Minnie Miyatake on trikes.

Photo by Toyo Miyatake, courtesy of Toyo Miyatake Studio

My brother and I spent our days walking around the perimeter of the camp, looking out at the highway and watching the cars go by and spending time with friends until school was finally established in October. My neighborhood friends...were sent to other camps, so it was a major disappointment not to be reunited with them.

—Momo Nagano, age 16 when she arrived at Manzanar

By July 1942, Manzanar had eighty baseball teams, with most games taking place in the firebreaks between blocks of barracks.

Photo by Dorothea Lange, courtesy of the National Archives and Records Administration

We met new friends from throughout the camp. To this day I have friends who were in the same class as me.

—Nob Kamibayashi

Photo by Toyo Miyatake, courtesy of Toyo Miyatake Studio

Photo by Toyo Miyatake, courtesy of Toyo Miyatake Studio

Our typical day was, as I remember, getting up, [then] we each had the responsibility to make our bed. We each had the responsibility to brush our teeth, wash our faces. We would go to the mess hall where we would have our meals, and then we would return to just be kids.

—Dennis Tojo Bambauer, age 7 when he arrived at Manzanar's Children's Village

[We went to the co-op] for ice cream and soda pop,...a haircut, [to have] our shoes repaired, or buy a new pair of shoes....As kids, we really went through shoes.

—Saburo Sasaki, age 7 when he arrived at Manzanar

Memorial Day, May 1942.
Photo by Francis Stewart, courtesy of the National Archives and Records Administration

A baseball game, July 1942.

Photo by Dorothea Lange, courtesy of the National Archives and Records Administration

Memorial Day, May 1942.

Photo by Francis Stewart, courtesy of the National Archives and Records Administration

Boy Scouts lead the Memorial Day parade alongside members of the American Legion, May 1942.

Photo by Francis Stewart, courtesy of the Library of Congress

Boy Scout Frank Kikuchi plays taps at Memorial Day services, May 1942.

Photo by Francis Stewart, courtesy of the National Archives and Records Administration

Yeah, I was with Troop 145 at Maryknoll [a Catholic school in the Little Tokyo area of Los Angeles]. I was a Star Scout and I was in a senior group. At the outbreak of war, I was a junior assistant scoutmaster, and also a bugler. I remember I used to blow the bugle calls when there were the district meetings....I had brought [to camp] my pretty brand new uniform...long, gray khaki pants and a heavy shirt, and I took it...'cause it's practical. And, hey, what do you know? [Memorial] Day, 1942, the administration called for a flag ceremony and they wanted somebody to blow taps....You can tell everybody's got their head down, all the other scouts and the flagbearers have their heads bowed down, so I know it's taps.

—Frank Kikuchi, age 17 when he arrived at Manzanar

Toy Loan Library

When large families were crowded in a single room, the child's play life was limited because of lack of physical space. The sixteen dollars per month earned by the family head would not [be enough to] go around to buy personal necessities, much less to buy play material for the younger children.

The Toy Loan Library provides an opportunity for children to borrow toys, play with them, and return the toys as they would their library books.

—Dr. Genevieve W. Carter, Superintendent of Education, June 1944

Children wait their turn at the Toy Loan Library.

Photo by Toyo Miyatake, courtesy of Toyo Miyatake Studio

Unearthed Treasures

The museum collection belonging to Manzanar National Historic Site comprises small treasures unearthed onsite during archaeological excavations, as well as personal belongings donated to the National Park Service by former internees, camp staff, and others. In 2010, Manzanar launched an online virtual museum on its website, http://www.nps.gov/manz.

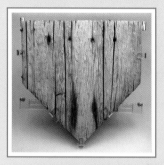

This wooden home plate was used in Manzanar's main baseball diamond, on the northeast side of camp. "Without baseball," recalls one internee, "life at Manzanar would have been miserable."

Toy soldier.

Baseball glove.

Marbles.

Toy tank.

"Someone in the fire department must have ordered...a red army helmet and painted [on] 'Manzanar Fire Dept mascot.' They gave [it] to me because I guess I hung around the station quite a bit."—Arthur Yamada

Blanket knitted by Mrs. Tomita for Lynne Sugimoto, the daughter of Anna Uta and Dan Shigeru Sugimoto, born at Manzanar on June 16, 1943.

Toy jacks.

Toy gun.

Toy cannon.

Kendo men and *do* (helmet and breastplate) once used in the *dojo* near Block 10 at Manzanar.

Memorial Day, May 1942.

Photo by Francis Stewart, courtesy of the National Archives and Records Administration

I really loved to find those doodlebugs. I don't know if you know what a doodlebug is, but it's kind of a fat little insect with two little pincers. What they do is they make a little trap, and by shaking they get this flying dust that's a conical shape. Of course, when an unsuspecting ant crawls in over the edge, it falls in there and it can't get out because the sand is so fine. It just crumbles under them trying to get out, and there's a doodlebug sitting at the bottom....We used to collect doodlebugs and put them in a box and watch them make their own little traps. Then we'd bring ants and toss them in there.

—Arthur Yamada

Playing near a nursery school, May 1942.

Photo by Francis Stewart, courtesy of the National Archives and Records Administration

Photo by Francis Stewart, courtesy of the National Archives and Records Administration

Manzanar was also a huge marble playground. I remember I had some beautiful marbles, but [then] didn't when I played with the older guys. The idea was to play with guys who weren't too good at it and win their marbles. Then the big guys would challenge us and take what we had. I remember the good players would come to our block like gunfighters and challenge us to play. None of us in our block was too good at this game, and we must have donated a lot of good marbles to those visiting players.

—Victor Muraoka, age 9 when
he arrived at Manzanar

The library, July 1, 1942.

Photo by Dorothea Lange, courtesy of the National Archives and Records Administration

Eventually some volunteer ladies...and I am sure there was men too...started organizing some classes at these recreation halls. My mother insisted I go.

—Nob Kamibayashi, commenting on school classes beginning during summer 1942

Photo by Toyo Miyatake, courtesy of Toyo Miyatake Studio

I don't know how we survived through that summer, going to school, walking to school, summer school, or even in our own barracks. It was very, very hot.

—Rose Honda, age 15 when she arrived at Manzanar

Photo by Ansel Adams, courtesy of the Library of Congress

In summer 1942, classes start on a voluntary basis, with minimal space, supplies, and staff. By the fall semester, barracks house more formal classrooms.

Photo by Dorothea Lange, courtesy of the National Archives and Records Administration

There were no desks. They had put tarpaper [and] linoleum on the floor. It was very cold in fall, and I remember those [days] first. I don't know how many months we sat on the floor; and then I find that there were only a few desks only for teachers. Eventually, you know, they caught up to us and got us desks and things and it became more and more normal.

—Chiyeko "Chickie" Hiraoka Matoba, age 15 when she arrived at Manzanar

Grade school fire drill in
Block 16, 1943.

Photo by Toyo Miyatake, courtesy of
Toyo Miyatake Studio

First grade class and teacher, 1943.

Photo by Toyo Miyatake, courtesy of Toyo Miyatake Studio

Choir practice, 1943.

Photo by Ansel Adams, courtesy of the Library of Congress

At the Children's Village, 1942.

Photo by Dorothea Lange, courtesy of the National Archives and Records Administration

It's always difficult to get up in front of the class. I had to, at that young age, come up with something to say or a story to tell every week. My reference material became comic books. I would take a comic book and read a comic strip, and then with the six or eight frames I would have to make a story up that would fit that and be able to tell a story. So, kind of, comic books saved my life, to be able to get up in front of the class and tell stories.

—Arthur Yamada

From Broadway-style musicals to traditional Japanese dances, performances and pageants reflect the bicultural nature of life in camp.

Photo by Toyo Miyatake, courtesy of Toyo Miyatake Studio

Louis Frizzell did it again! Bouquets are in line for another of his successful productions. It seems this young "DeMille" has really earned a reputation for himself with one successful event after another, since he took over the duties here as "melody master" and dramatic instructor. His last big production here, the Senior Play, was close to the climactic event of his brilliant career in Manzanar.

—*Valediction, 1945*, yearbook of the Associated Student Body of Manzanar High School

Japanese *Obon* festival; Minnie Miyatake (photographer Toyo's daughter) is pictured at the far right.

Photo by Toyo Miyatake, courtesy of Toyo Miyatake Studio

Music teacher Louis Frizzell (*far left*) and choir in the Manzanar auditorium.

Photo by Toyo Miyatake, courtesy of Toyo Miyatake Studio

Members of the Dusty Chicks softball team: *(left to right)* May Noma, unidentified, Ritsuko Masuda, Fuji Kuwahara, Rosie Maruki Kakuuchi, Yoshiko "Peewee" Kusunoki Nakamura, Masa Fujioka Kunitomi, and Marian Fuji. (Figure at far right is unidentified.)
Photo by Francis Stewart, courtesy of the National Archives and Records Administration

School was sort of [the] center of my activities; and so was sports. There were a lot of sports.

—Chiyeko "Chickie" Hiraoka Matoba

Baton practice, Florence Kuwata, 1943.
Photo by Ansel Adams, courtesy of the Library of Congress

Volleyball, 1943.

Photo by Ansel Adams, courtesy of the Library of Congress

I wasn't bored. It was just being free to do whatever I wanted to do, and primarily to play. I went to school. I was a fairly good student in school, had no problems there. But camp to me was like—I can't describe it. I was free. I could do whatever I wanted to do, and that was all in sports.

—Ted Ikeda, age 12 when he arrived at Manzanar

Manzanar 'A' League Champ, 1943.

Photo from Yuri Yamazaki Matsunaga, courtesy of Manzanar National Historic Site

Basketball game, February 1943.

Photo by Francis Stewart, courtesy of the National Archives and Records Administration

Manzanar football game.

Photo from the Maeda family, courtesy of Manzanar National Historic Site

The *judo dojo* at Manzanar, 1943.

Photo from Kayoko Wakita, courtesy of Manzanar National
Historic Site

The Forget-Me-Nots: *(back row, left to right)* Aya Nishi, Betty Yamada, Mary
Matsuno, Cherry Yamada, Yuki Shiba, and Miyo Nishi; *(front, left to right)* Toshi
Akemoto, Grace Araishi, Harumi Hino (advisor), Michi Yoshimoto, and Mary Honda.

Courtesy of Manzanar National Historic Site

(Back row, left to right) Haruki Murakami, Roy Izumita, and Hank Harada; (front row, left to right) Arnold Maeda and Takeo Sato.

Photo from the Maeda family, courtesy of Manzanar National Historic Site

I worked on the farm since I was seven years old, and when they put us in camps I didn't have to work no more. So I can't say every-thing was bad. And also, I met a lot of young, good-looking girls. Hey, I was a teenager, I was fifteen, I noticed those things. So I can't say everything was bad, but I still don't like the idea of losing my freedom. That is no fun for anybody.

—Paul Norihiro, age 15 when he arrived at Manzanar

(Left to right) Diane Tani, Amy Iwaki, Kiyo Yoshida, Mae Kageyama, and Yoneko Kodama.

Photo from Mae Kageyama Kakehashi, courtesy of Manzanar National Historic Site

You know, they would have to have a war just before my prom. I'm looking forward to this prom all these years.... When you're a teenager, you don't think beyond [yourself], or deep enough. You're thinking about yourself, what you're missing out....That meant a lot to me to go to a junior prom, and I didn't go.

—Mary Suzuki Ichino, age 18 when she arrived at Manzanar

Young women practice the baton in hopes of becoming majorettes, 1944.
Photo by Toyo Miyatake, courtesy of Toyo Miyatake Studio

(Left to right) Tak Shinto, Haruki Murakami, Yosh Shishido, Takeo Sato, Seiichi Torii, and Arnold Maeda.
Photo from Mae Kageyama Kakehashi, courtesy of Manzanar National Historic Site

Dances—yes. This was during the swing era!

—Mas Okui

Photo by Francis Stewart, courtesy of the National Archives and Records Administration

The Sierra Stars.
Photo from Jack and Peggy Iwata, courtesy of the Japanese American National Museum (93.102.138)

Grace Maruki, 1944.
Photo from the Minato family, courtesy of Manzanar National Historic Site

Halloween dance.
Photo by Toyo Miyatake, courtesy of Toyo Miyatake Studio

Below: Margie Shimizu Hiroshima, the "Queen of Manzanar," 1942.
Photo from Jack and Peggy Iwata, courtesy of the Japanese American National Museum (93.102.133)

I remember a beautiful girl in our class....I sat next to her in class. She was pretty in face but what impressed me most was her beautiful handwriting. She wrote as if her hand was moved by mystic influences. The time I remember most was when I tried to write like her. I had a thick black art pencil and sharpened it to a needle point. When I wrote, it looked as if I used a crayon. This beautiful girl took my pencil and showed me she could write as well with any implement.

—Raymond Muraoka, age 6 when he arrived at Manzanar

Playing with ice at the picnic grounds.

Photo by Toyo Miyatake, courtesy of Toyo Miyatake Studio

From *Our World, 1943–44*, the Manzanar High School yearbook.

Photo by Toyo Miyatake, courtesy of Toyo Miyatake Studio

I grew up with boys, so boys were always around me. I was a tomboy. I grew up, you know, climbing trees and playing baseball. I was very comfortable with boys, so I always had a boyfriend.

—Chiyeko "Chickie" Hiraoka Matoba

There was no place to go. If you wanted to take your girlfriend somewhere, go a mile that way, a mile that way, a mile that way, and a mile that way, you got to a barbed wire fence.

—Mas Okui

Sons and brothers serving in the U.S. military occasionally visited family and friends still confined in Manzanar. Altogether, 174 young men and women from Manzanar served in the armed forces during World War II. Left, high school friends Kazue Shibuya and Katsumi Taniguchi visit at Bairs Creek, a popular picnic site.

Photo by Katsumi Taniguchi, courtesy of Manzanar National Historic Site

Brother and sister George and Kazue Shibuya face a guard tower.

Photo by Katsumi Taniguchi, courtesy of Manzanar National Historic Site

I never had girlfriends. We were thinking constantly about sports. Don't get me wrong, there were girls that you'd see you liked, but you don't have guts enough to say, "Where do you want to go in camp?" Some guys knew how to do it, but I couldn't. Holding hands, you know, I'd be embarrassed if I'm holding hands and my friends see me holding hands. So I never did.

—Tamotsu Isozaki, age 15 when he arrived at Manzanar's Children's Village

AN EVOLVING COMMUNITY

Manzanar changed substantially between the day it opened in March 1942 and the day it closed in November 1945. Outdoors, internees transformed the desert landscape with ponds and gardens. Indoors, sheet rock insulated the rough pine board walls and ceilings of most barracks apartments, while linoleum covered the floorboards. Gradually people accumulated collections of handmade furniture, belongings sent up from storage in Los Angeles, and new catalog purchases from Montgomery Ward and Sears, Roebuck, and Co. During the three and a half years Manzanar operated, couples courted and married, families welcomed babies and mourned deaths, and young men and women went off to colleges, jobs, and the armed services.

Communities developed within Manzanar's thirty-six blocks. Each block consisted of fourteen barracks, communal men's and women's latrines, a mess hall, a recreation building, and a laundry room and ironing room. At first, Manzanar's cookie-cutter-style blocks appeared identical, but over time they evolved into distinct neighborhoods. Pleasure and "victory" gardens, basketball and volleyball courts, baseball diamonds, playground and gymnastics equipment—all of it built by internees—altered the high desert landscape. A few blocks maintained their prewar community ties; Blocks 9, 10, and 11 were for Terminal Islanders from San Pedro, California, and Block 3 housed Bainbridge Islanders from Washington State (most of whom later transferred to Minidoka War Relocation Center in February 1943). Many other blocks brought strangers together, however, housing San Fernando Valley truck farmers alongside Little Tokyo merchants from Los Angeles, and Christians from Florin next to Buddhists from Beverly Hills.

The WRA's goal of self-sufficiency for all of the camps was substantially met by the internees' labor on farms and in mess halls, classrooms, and hospitals. Manzanar's 440 acres of farmland supplied fresh produce, and its chicken ranch, hog farm, and cattle herd provided fresh eggs and meat. The pay scale ranged from twelve to nineteen dollars per month per employee, a rate that specifically prevented Japanese Americans from earning more than a private in the U.S. Army (twenty-one dollars per month from 1942 to 1945).

Block 23 group portrait. In all, 541 babies came into the world at Manzanar; sixteen infants and eleven children died within its confines.

Photo by Toyo Miyatake, courtesy of Toyo Miyatake Studio

Panorama of Block 12 residents, mess hall, and pond.

Photo by Toyo Miyatake, courtesy of Toyo Miyatake Studio

Panorama of Block 30 residents, 1944.

Photo from Bill Taketa, courtesy of Manzanar
National Historic Site

Photo from Jack and Peggy Iwata, courtesy of the
Japanese American National Museum (102.123)

View from a barracks window.

Photo by Katsumi Taniguchi, courtesy of Manzanar National Historic Site

Bride and groom Roselyn Takahashi and Yoshio Maruyama with their wedding party, October 10, 1942.

Photo from Mae Kageyama Kakehashi, courtesy of Manzanar National Historic Site

I remember my mother's friends who had gotten married just before we came to camp so they wouldn't be separated. It always seemed odd to me, in the middle of the heat of the afternoon, that this young couple, this beautiful girl and her husband, would always tell us kids, "You got to be quiet now because we're going to take a nap." Well, as I've grown up, I think there were other reasons, but to our youthful ears, a nap was sufficient.

—Mas Okui, age 10 when he arrived at Manzanar

Photo by Toyo Miyatake, courtesy of
Toyo Miyatake Studio

My baby sister Grace, whom I cradled in my arms
under a jacket against the cold night air and the
swirling dust, was just fifty-three days old that
windy, fateful first night in Manzanar.

—George Atsushi Matsumoto, age 17 when he
arrived at Manzanar

Photo by Toyo Miyatake, courtesy of
Toyo Miyatake Studio

Funeral of Ruby Maruki Watanabe and her twin daughters, Diane and Sachiko, August 1942. In one of the worst hospital tragedies at Manzanar, Ruby succumbed to hemorrhaging during childbirth. According to Ruby's family, Dr. James Goto failed to call in a specialist to help with a difficult delivery. Ruby and Sachiko died on August 15; Diane the next day. The community mourned soon after. Ruby's father, Shinkichi Maruki, later superimposed Ruby's 1939 wedding portrait *(upper left)* on a memorial photograph taken by Toyo Miyatake.

Photo by Toyo Miyatake, courtesy of Rosie Maruki Kakuuchi

Top left: One of the Takenaka children.

Photo by Toyo Miyatake, courtesy of Toyo Miyatake Studio

Top right: Donny Mariguchi and trike, June 13, 1943.

Photo from the Yanai family, courtesy of Manzanar National Historic Site

Left: Photo by Dorothea Lange, courtesy of the National Archives and Records Administration

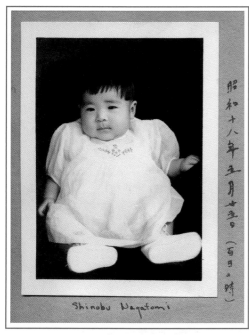

Shinobu Nagatomi, one hundred days old, May 25, 1943.

Photo from the Hosoi family, courtesy of Manzanar
National Historic Site

Outside a barracks door.

Photo from the Hosoi family, courtesy of Manzanar National Historic Site

Family photo album.

Photos from the Hosoi family, courtesy of Manzanar National Historic Site

Julia Hirosawa with stuffed panda and puppy, 1943.

Photos from the Hirosawa family, courtesy of Manzanar
National Historic Site

The Miyatake family celebrates the 1943 holidays in their barracks apartment: (*left to right*) Bobby, Richard, Archie, Hiro (mother), Minnie, and Toyo Miyatake (father).

Photo by Ansel Adams, courtesy of the Library of Congress

I don't remember whether it was Christmas or whether it was New Year's, but one of my fond memories was the wonderful *sushi* that was brought to camp, and the *mochi* balls. What I remember is not how good they were, but [that] they became missiles. We kids would gather up and pretend like we were taking it to eat and then we would get out onto the grass area, and they became missiles. We threw 'em at each other and we ran and tried to dodge them and so forth.

—Dennis Tojo Bambauer, age 7 when he arrived at Manzanar's Children's Village

Halloween, 1944.

Photo by Toyo Miyatake, courtesy of Toyo Miyatake Studio

Santa comes to Manzanar, 1944.

Photo by Toyo Miyatake, courtesy of Toyo Miyatake Studio

Christmas of 1942, we had no money. All the kids went to their block's recreation hall. There was a Santa Claus and gifts. Each kid got one gift. I didn't think I would get anything. Here I was, an eleven-year-old, getting a coloring book with water paints from some kid in Iowa [through a church donation program]. I wrote a thank-you letter to that kid.

—Mas Okui

At Christmas, various religious groups brought modest gifts and candy for children, and we managed to have a mess hall party with a dress-up Santa Claus. Everyone put on a brave face for the children, but Christmas was the saddest time of the year.

—Wilbur Sato, age 13 when he arrived at Manzanar

Above: Christmas pageant, 1944.

Photo from Mary Suzuki Ichino, courtesy of Manzanar National Historic Site

Photo by Toyo Miyatake, courtesy of Toyo Miyatake Studio

Birthday party in a barracks.

Courtesy of Manzanar National Historic Site

Photo by Toyo Miyatake, courtesy
of Toyo Miyatake Studio

Photo by Toyo Miyatake, courtesy
of Toyo Miyatake Studio

Hospital School

Several dozen children received educational instruction at the Hospital School, designed specifically for those whose health conditions or disabilities required skilled medical care or constant supervision. Some attended these classes temporarily, while they recuperated from surgery, for instance, whereas others attended regularly, including those who required special education services, like the three children with hearing impairments.

Eleanor Thomas, a Special Class teacher, described "A Typical School Day" in the Hospital School:

The discrepancy in age does not hamper the [schooling] procedure. Our "younger" group includes a severely handicapped nineteen-year-old boy, who is "enjoying" his first school experience with the same enthusiasm of the little ones. There has always been a fine, cooperative spirit among all the children, the older helping the younger ones, the less handicapped the more handicapped, the ambulatory the bed and wheelchair children. They have accepted each other naturally and without question. Whether it is a gardening unit, or the farm, or stores that we have chosen for our unit, there is something that even the smallest child can work on with interest during the Social Studies period....

By now the ambulance has arrived to take home for lunch the children for whom a full school day is too long. One little boy lies down for his pre-lunch nap, and the rest go outside for their play period.

All photographs on the facing page courtesy of Manzanar National Historic Site

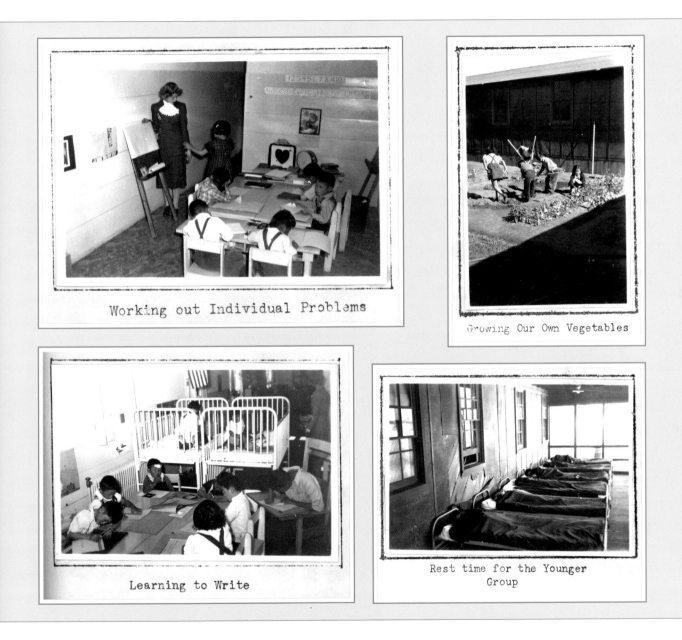

Working out Individual Problems

Growing Our Own Vegetables

Learning to Write

Rest time for the Younger
Group

Children's Village

From 1942 to 1945 the Children's Village at Manzanar housed a total of 101 children, many of whom had been removed from foster homes and orphanages up and down the West Coast. Some had been orphaned before the war (and some of those were living with white foster parents), and a few had been separated from their parents when the latter were detained by the FBI in Department of Justice camps shortly after war broke out. During the war, some infants born to unwed mothers at other camps were also, for varying reasons, sent to the Children's Village.

The War Relocation Authority (WRA) sought to reunite children with parents confined in other camps, and to find foster homes or adoptive families for many of the other children, but it succeeded in placing only a few before the war ended. At the time, California's adoption practices did not favor placing children with parents of a different race.

Manzanar's Children's Village was actually built as a direct result of requests from social workers Harry and Lillian Matsumoto, who managed the Shonien Japanese Children's Home in Los Angeles before the war. Lillian recalls that the U.S. Army thought children "could be dispersed like the rest of the people," so to prevent that the Matsumotos encouraged the government to build "separate quarters" for orphans. The result was an orphanage at Manzanar: the Children's Village. The core population of the facility was comprised of orphans from three institutions—Shonien, the Salvation Army Japanese Children's Home in San Francisco, and the Maryknoll Home for Japanese Children in Los Angeles—and Lillian and Harry Matsumoto became the directors.

When children from these three institutions came together at Manzanar, significant age differences posed difficulties at first. As Taeko Kajiwara Nagayama remembers, "When we [from Shonien] went to the Children's Village and merged with the Salvation Army children, I first thought, 'Boy, they're rough!...Because the children, or the boys, I guess you'd say, from the Salvation Army were much bigger, older teenagers...and our kids were more or less younger....But they seemed very friendly after we got to know them."

Children living in the Village nevertheless learned and played with other children in camp despite occasional teasing, or feelings of being outsiders. From Lillian Matsumoto's perspective, "We encouraged the older children...to make friends with other children in Manzanar....They would be going to the same schools, attending church, and so forth. But we did restrict one thing[:]...that, at every meal, they should come back to the Village."

Infants of the Children's Village, 1942.

Photo by Dorothea Lange, courtesy of the National Archives and Records Administration

Life in the Village was simple. After rising in the morning, we made our beds and straightened up our quarters before going to breakfast. After breakfast we did our chores, then went to school. After school we were free until dinner. During this time we were allowed to associate with the other children in camp, and made many "outside" friends.

—Clara Seno Hayashi, age 18 when she arrived at Manzanar's Children's Village

The most important thing to a kid of five years old is other children. It's not the place or anything like that. That's not what's important; it's if you have friends to play with...not what kind of castle we're about to enter. So the important thing was, "Oh, good, we can get out and run! We can be with our friends! We can go to the bathroom!"...I remember we had little cots, and we had our own little space that they fixed with a box to put our personal things in....It might have been a crate for all I know, standing up like a dresser. We all had our private little space with our private things.

—Celeste Loi Teodor, age 6 when she arrived at Manzanar's Children's Village

Children's Village residents and staff, Easter 1944; Celeste Loi Teodor is pictured in the second row, fourth from left.

Photo by Toyo Miyatake, courtesy of Toyo Miyatake Studio

George Ganase wears his first clothing allotment, a surplus World War I uniform.

Courtesy of the Lillian Matsumoto Private Collection

The first allotment [of clothing the WRA] gave to the children at the Children's Village because winter was coming....Do you know what it was? Old World War I soldiers' outfits.

—Lillian Matsumoto, director of Manzanar's Children's Village

[It was] a very lonely place with babies crying and nothing to do. It was like the end of the world for me.

—Francis L. Honda, age 7 when she arrived at Manzanar's Children's Village

I liked the babies and used to climb up on stools to peer into their cribs and play like I was taking care of them.

—Annie Shiraishi Sakamoto, age 3 when she arrived at Manzanar's Children's Village

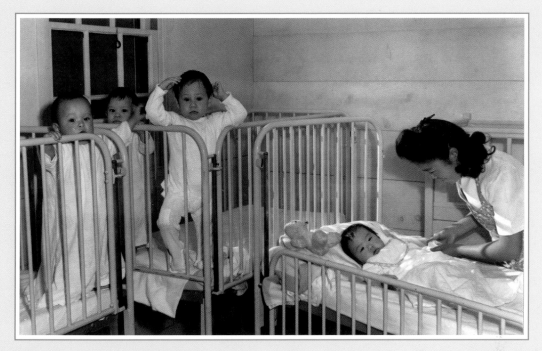

Photo by Ansel Adams, courtesy of the Library of Congress

When it's dark and the searchlights are coming in through the window every so often, I was trying to think what was happening there, why these searchlights. Maybe they were doing that because they were watching us or afraid that we would do something wrong, like maybe run away. I must have been insecure because I would wet the bed at night, so of course, naturally, the people who were taking care of us would have to clean it up.

—Annie Shiraishi Sakamoto

Playing with a bunny at the Children's Village; Harry Matsumoto *(far left)* runs the Village with his wife, Lillian.
Photo by Toyo Miyatake, courtesy of Toyo Miyatake Studio

Courtesy of the Lillian Matsumoto Private Collection

Free at last. Happy? Why, naturally. After weeks of isolation because of [the] measles and chicken pox quarantine, the energetic children of the Children's Village are once again free to roam about with their friends.

—*Manzanar Free Press*, August 21, 1942

At Children's Village, 1942.

Photo by Dorothea Lange, courtesy of the National Archives and Records
Administration

Identification card for Dennis Tojo Bambauer.
Courtesy of Manzanar National Historic Site

When I got ready to leave camp,...I was called and told...that I was leaving to go live with the Bambauers, and ultimately I was adopted by them. I was told that I had to stop by the officers'—the military compound—before I could leave. And the purpose of them, or my stop, was so that I could be fingerprinted, and I'm six, seven years old, and I remember the soldier saying, "This is in case you do anything bad; we'll be able to catch you." That was a traumatic experience for me, and I'm sure that the soldier didn't mean anything of that, but it really knocked me for a loop. I was really sad. It didn't make me angry because at that age you don't get angry. You get scared. So it just made me even more scared. I didn't know what I was. I didn't know where I was going. I didn't know anything about the Bambauers except that they had come to the camp and they wanted to adopt a child and so they selected me.

—Dennis Tojo Bambauer, age 7 when he arrived at Manzanar's Children's Village

CONFINEMENT and CONFLICT

Although their citizenship status did not protect them from being sent to camp in the first place, it did qualify some young adults for different treatment once inside. For a brief six-month period, they could work in the relatively well-paying camouflage net factory at Manzanar, whereas their non-citizen parents could not. Protests from some *Issei* leaders over the pay scale—more than the maximum nineteen dollars per month offered for the WRA jobs they were eligible for—contributed to the WRA's decision to cancel the project. The net factory also sparked intergenerational debate about the ethics of supporting the war effort from behind barbed wire. "At first I worked at a camouflage place," recalls Paul Norihiro. "But then they cut that down shortly thereafter because some of the elders started saying, 'Why are we making camouflage nets when our country puts [us] into concentration camps?' So they stopped it." After the factory closed, fifteen-year-old Paul drove a government vehicle to deliver supplies to crews installing drywall and linoleum in the barracks. Other teens worked as dishwashers and cooks' assistants in mess halls, earning from twelve to sixteen dollars per month.

Generational differences between many *Nisei* and their more traditional parents figured in matters large and small. "A problem...arose out of conflict in food tastes between the...first-generation Japanese and their American-born children," explained Manzanar's Chief Steward, Joseph Winchester. "The older people were accustomed to, and desired, larger amounts of rice and Japanese food." More profound differences came to the surface during the Manzanar riot and loyalty questionnaire crises, when citizen children often held different perspectives than their foreign-national parents. *Issei* mother Shino Bannai felt the effects of this generational divide acutely: "The pain I felt in the shameful experience of camp was for my children rather than for myself. The laws of the U.S. prevented us from becoming citizens, but my children had been born and raised here and were always told to be good Americans."

THE MANZANAR RIOT

The community suffered its gravest crisis on December 6, 1942, when tensions that had simmered since March finally reached the boiling point. One of the Manzanar riot's innocent victims was seventeen-year-old James Ito, whom a classmate recalled as "a quiet boy who seldom went out at night." But on the evening of December 6, 1942, he joined several hundred others near the Manzanar police station, where mess hall chef and kitchen-workers organizer Harry Ueno was under arrest for allegedly beating Fred Tayama, a past chapter president of the Japanese American Citizen's League and a rumored FBI informant. Eight months of confinement, grievances against the WRA and suspected informers, and rumors of black marketing of sugar and meat fueled the crowd's anger. The WRA called in the military police, and 135 soldiers deployed in a line of skirmish attempted, albeit unsuccessfully, to disperse the crowd with tear gas. As the crowd scattered in chaos, someone pushed an unoccupied vehicle toward the soldiers. Two soldiers fired into the crowd, instantly killing James Ito. Jim Kanagawa, age twenty-one, died five days later, and ten others were injured. In the days that followed, eighty-one internees were removed from the camp, either for their own protection or to isolate those the WRA considered "troublemakers."

"LOYALTY" AND LEAVING CAMP

Despite the significant U.S. victory at the Battle of Midway in June 1942 and the subsequently increased public optimism about the war against Japan, the WRA continued to implement the forced removal of Japanese and Japanese Americans from the West Coast during the summer months of that year. By the time Manzanar approached its peak population, in September 1942, a growing number of WRA administrators believed that tens of thousands of loyal U.S. citizens should no longer be deprived of their liberty. As noted in the *Washington Post,* "American democracy and the Constitution of the United States are too vital to be ignored....The panic of Pearl Harbor is now past." Acting jointly, the War Department and WRA then began a program to distinguish the "loyal" from the "disloyal." The War Department sought to clear *Nisei* for voluntary service in the armed forces, and the WRA hoped to pave the way for resettling Japanese Americans out of the camps, in part to avoid any more conflicts like the Manzanar riot, which both the WRA and U.S. government viewed as a clash between pro-American and pro-Japanese factions in the camp. However, the loyalty questionnaires they used, intended to rush the release of people, instead ushered in a period of chaos and crisis at all ten camps.

As the government forced internees to "declare their loyalty," private sentiments about the camp experience suddenly became very public issues with profound consequences. Different choices led to different fates: jobs and colleges in the Midwest and on the East Coast, military service in Europe, segregation at the Tule Lake camp, or deportation to Japan. A total of 913 *Nisei* men from Manzanar answered "no" to two key questions on the loyalty questionnaire, and although the reasons for their responses varied, the U.S. government considered each negative respondent "disloyal" and later sent these "no-no boys" and others from Manzanar to the Tule Lake Segregation Center, in Northern California. A fourth-grade student explained why he had to leave Manzanar for Tule Lake: "Teacher, my big brother answered 'no' on the loyalty question so our family can go to Tule Lake together and not be separated. So, I'm not an American anymore."

By March 1944 the WRA had transferred nearly 2,200 people from Manzanar to Tule Lake. They went for many different reasons. Some spouses, children, and siblings went along to keep their families together. Many *Nisei* felt obligated to help aging parents regain a foothold after the war rather than risk their lives in battle, and being sent to Tule Lake was one way to ensure they survived to do that. Some people had property and relatives back in Japan to consider, and some expressed loyalty to Japan either out of resentment for their treatment at the hands of the U.S. government or because they truly hoped Japan would win the war. Others simply weren't ready or able to move to unfamiliar, potentially hostile places outside California and preferred segregation at Tule Lake instead.

UNCOMMON VALOR

> We...literally ran—the three miles to the draft board, stringing back over the streets and sidewalks, jostling for position, like a bunch of marathoners gone berserk.
>
> —U.S. Senator Daniel K. Inouye, on *Nisei* enlistment in the Army's 442nd Regimental Combat Team in Hawaii, 1943

For a few young men and women, serving in the U.S. military provided a means to leave camp.

Approximately 4,000 Japanese American men and women went into military service directly from War Relocation Centers, including 2,800 who were drafted. In November 1942, Karl Yoneda left Manzanar with twelve others to join the Military Intelligence Service (MIS). A few months later, Burns Arikawa volunteered for the 442nd from Manzanar, joining his brothers Frank and James in the service. In December 1943, Iris Watanabe left Amache to volunteer for the Women's Auxiliary Army Corps (WAAC). Kazuo Ono, an *Issei* from Minidoka, tried several times to join the army, a goal he finally reached in March 1945, after the Selective Service allowed voluntary induction of *Issei*. Together, these Japanese Americans and thousands of others proved U.S. Army Air Force Sergeant Ben Kuroki's words: "Under fire, a man's ancestry, what he did before the war,...don't matter at all[;]...whether you realize it at the time or not, you're living and proving democracy."

Several thousand *Nisei* soldiers helped defend Hawaii during Japan's attack on Pearl Harbor. However, as military leaders and others in Washington, D.C., continued to question the loyalty of all Japanese Americans, most were transferred to a new segregated unit, the Hawaiian Provisional Infantry Battalion, which was sent in June 1942 to train at Camp McCoy, Wisconsin, and later formed the core of the 100th Infantry Battalion. In 1943, when the army announced the formation of the all-*Nisei* 442nd Regimental Combat Team, volunteer turnout in Hawaii—where most of the Japanese American population had not been relocated into camps—far exceeded expectations, while that on the mainland lagged far behind.

Several factors led to the formation of the all-*Nisei* 442nd Regimental Combat Team. One was that the 100th Infantry Battalion from Hawaii, then training at Camp Shelby in Mississippi, impressed military leaders with their "go for broke" valor. At the same time, leaders of the Japanese American Citizens League (JACL) lobbied aggressively in Washington, D.C., arguing that the only way to change public opinion was to demonstrate that *Nisei* would die for their country. By January 1943, Secretary of War Henry L. Stimson firmly backed the creation of an all-*Nisei* unit, stating, "Loyalty is a voice that must be heard."

Although no young men from Manzanar chose to resist the draft, several hundred from other camps did, particularly at Heart Mountain War Relocation Center in Wyoming. Led by *Nisei* Kiyoshi Okamoto, draft resisters at Heart Mountain organized as the Fair Play Committee (FPC), stating that they would willingly serve their country once their rights as citizens were restored. "The Constitution...is not a mere scrap of paper," FPC spokesman Frank Emi wrote in response to a *Heart Mountain Sentinel* editorial calling the resisters "whimpering weaklings...afraid to prove themselves." Authorities branded Okamoto and fellow FPC leader Sam Horino "troublemakers" and sent them to Tule Lake Segregation Center. With Frank Emi and four other FPC leaders, they were tried and sentenced to up to four years in prison, although their convictions on conspiracy charges were reversed on appeal in late 1945. Another eighty-five Heart Mountain resisters were arrested and tried in two separate mass trials, and many of them were found guilty of violating the Selective Service Act and sentenced to up to three years in prison. In 1947, President Harry S. Truman pardoned all wartime draft resisters, yet draft resistance remained a divisive issue within the Japanese American community for decades.

All told, an estimated 315 *Nisei* men refused military induction, and 263 were convicted on federal charges of draft evasion. Some were fined one penny; others served sentences in federal prison. In contrast, Judge Louis Goodman dismissed the charges against 27 resisters from Tule Lake, stating, "It is shocking to the conscience that an American citizen be confined on the ground of disloyalty, and then...be compelled to serve in the armed forces, or be prosecuted."

RESETTLEMENT AND RELOCATION

Beginning in June 1942 the WRA granted permission for some internees to leave camp. After being investigated and cleared on an individual basis, they were allowed to move east to work or attend college. With more freedom than families with young children or elderly adults, young people typically left first. By the end of the war, a total of 40,000 people had left for colleges and jobs in the Midwest or on the East Coast, and several thousand had joined the military. Hundreds of people were also allowed to go on temporary seasonal furloughs to help farmers harvest crops.

Nearly three years after removing Japanese Americans from their homes, the U.S. Army finally lifted the mass exclusion order in January 1945. When one teenager at Manzanar imagined life after camp and "going back in to public schools with Caucasians," she got "butterflies" in her stomach. By then, many *Nisei* had resettled in the Midwest and on the East Coast, and their parents had to decide whether to join their children in new communities or return to their prewar towns. Many had lost their homes, businesses, and farms and were forced to start over again. Because of that, some people chose to stay in camp as long as possible, uncertain of where or how to rebuild their lives.

A young farmworker, May 1942.

Photo by Francis Stewart, courtesy of the National Archives and Records Administration

I went to work in the lumberyard. You know the drywall they put inside the barracks? We did all the hauling. I was fifteen years old and I was driving a government vehicle.

—Paul Norihiro, age 15 when he arrived at Manzanar

The camouflage net factory operated for six months in 1942.

Photo by Dorothea Lange, courtesy of the National Archives and Records Administration

The best job I ever had was working at the "Caucasian" mess hall, where camp administrators ate. They paid for their meals (I guess) but the food there was a hell of a lot better than what we were getting in our mess hall. (I never saw them eat the "kabocha" that we had so many times in our mess hall.) The food was good, and we could take home a lot of stuff for our family. My job was washing dishes, sweeping, mopping, and helping the cooks. I worked there the longest and hated to leave....I started working when I was ten years old and worked until I was thirteen, when the camp closed.

—Victor Muraoka, age 9 when he arrived at Manzanar

International News Photo, University of Southern California Library, Department of Special Collections, Regional History Collection

I did not complete the whole eleventh grade. I said, "What am I going to school for?" They made you pledge allegiance and everything.

—Paul Norihiro

I was a senior. I was going to graduate in June, and I think it was April that [my father] died. What's interesting is nobody told me he was dying. My brothers and my mother knew…. Nobody tells girls anything in the Japanese culture. So one day I guess I figured out that he was, you know, dying; and I kind of really grew up. After he died I really grew up, and I said, "Wow, I'd better get out there and make a living for myself." This is why I left camp.

—Chiyeko "Chickie" Hiraoka Matoba, age 16 when she arrived at Manzanar

High school graduation, 1943.

Photo from Jack and Peggy Iwata, courtesy of the Japanese American National Museum (93.102.142)

George Nishimura, age seventeen, working at the Wakonda Country Club in Des Moines, Iowa, 1944.

Courtesy of the National Archives and Records Administration

All I can remember is the senior banquet. We held that in one of the mess halls, and what they served us was rabbit. I could never eat rabbit because when I was young we used to live on a farm and...they became like pets, but my father considered them food. Whenever he'd kill a rabbit, it was one of my pets, so I couldn't eat him. And that's what they served for our senior banquet. The fellow across from me, he was just devouring his, so I gave him mine. But that's about the only recollection I have about graduation, except for we were the first graduating class [to graduate in the auditorium]. Arnold Maeda was the valedictorian.

—Sam Ono, age 15 when he arrived at Manzanar

Exchanging goodbyes near the sentry post.

Photo by Ansel Adams, courtesy of the Library of Congress

Called "segregants" by the WRA, 2,165 people were transferred from Manzanar War Relocation Center to Tule Lake Segregation Center based on their responses to the loyalty questionnaire.

Courtesy of The Bancroft Library, University of California, Berkeley (Negative: 1967.014 v. 66 HG-573—PIC)

I never felt sorry that I was in Manzanar. I mean, I knew all the injustices, you know, as I got older and older, and also out of camp...you realize how ridiculous the whole thing was and how much we did miss out....As you get older...you realize how serious that situation was that should never happen again.

—Chiyeko "Chickie" Hiraoka Matoba

Photo by Ansel Adams, courtesy of the Library of Congress

Leaving, 1944.

Photo by Toyo Miyatake, courtesy of Toyo Miyatake Studio

Captain A. M. Branson, induction officer from the Ninth Command Recruiting and Induction District, swears Manzanar men into the Enlisted Reserve Corps on November 29, 1944.

Photo by Toyo Miyatake, courtesy of the Eastern California Museum

I think the government was really surprised when so few people actually volunteered [to join the army], but it was a year after we had been in camp. We had been confined for over a year, we had lost everything, and then they're asking the young men to turn around and go into the service, and I think many of them felt that they just couldn't do that. They were willing to serve if they would release their parents out of the camp.

—Sue Kunitomi Embrey, age 19 when she arrived at Manzanar

Soldier visiting his parents at Manzanar, 1944.

Photo by Toyo Miyatake, courtesy of
Toyo Miyatake Studio

Sergeant Victor Tierman explains the Selective Service
registration process to *Nisei* men age seventeen and older,
February 11, 1943.

Photo by Francis Stewart, courtesy of the National
Archives and Records Administration

You know, that question [on the loyalty question-naire] I realize now is so unfair, and I really don't know for sure how I answered....I was so mad, though, that they would dare to ask a question like that where it would tend to sort of break up a family....How could my father answer that question where he has to for-swear allegiance to the Japanese emperor....You can't forswear what you didn't have.

—Frank Kikuchi, age 17 when he arrived at Manzanar

Shizuko Fukuhara, 4, and her sister Yoshino, 2, play with two neighbor children in Farmingdale, Long Island, where their parents and grandparents relocated from Manzanar to work at the Calderone Greenhouses, 1945.

Photo by Stone Ishimaru, courtesy of The Bancroft Library, University of California, Berkeley (Negative: 1967.014 v. 40 EG-885—PIC)

Temporary housing for the Oshima family, Chicago, August 1943.

Photo by Charles Mace, courtesy of The Bancroft Library, University of California, Berkeley (Negative: 1967.014 v. 41 EH-035—PIC)

DISMANTLING MANZANAR

The last Japanese Americans left Manzanar on November 21, 1945, with a one-way ticket and twenty-five dollars provided by the WRA. They left behind barracks, ponds and gardens, dusty baseball diamonds, and enduring structures, including the sentry posts, cemetery monument, and auditorium. They took with them memories of life behind wire.

Manzanar War Relocation Center once had the Owens Valley's newest hospital, sewage treatment plant, and overall infrastructure. The U.S. government spent $4 million to construct Manzanar (and approximately $80 million on all ten camps), and recouped only a fraction of that cost by selling entire barracks and mess halls, scrap lumber, and used equipment after the war. Manzanar's hospital equipment was sold to the Northern Inyo Hospital in Bishop, and nearly two hundred Manzanar buildings were moved elsewhere in the Owens Valley to serve as homes, churches, motels, and meeting halls.

CERTAIN PRIVILEGES

> "You may think that the Constitution is your security—it is nothing but a piece of paper..., it is nothing at all, unless you have sound and uncorrupted public opinion."
>
> —Charles Evans Hughes, Chief Justice of the U.S. Supreme Court, 1930–1941

Ever since President Franklin D. Roosevelt signed Executive Order 9066, politicians, military leaders, legal scholars, and the American public have questioned whether war with Japan justified the exclusion of Japanese American citizens from their West Coast homes, businesses, and communities. At the heart of the debate rests the U.S. Constitution and the rights it defines for all Americans. Through a decades-long process of Supreme Court litigation, grassroots efforts, legal and academic scholarship, and ultimately reparations legislation, the case for the "military justification" of the forced removal has been summarily dismissed.

Even though President Roosevelt had privately concluded earlier in the year that confining American citizens violated both the spirit and the letter of the law, he delayed announcing his position until after the congressional elections of 1944. It was then—and belatedly for many—he stated, "It is felt by a great many lawyers that under the Constitution they [Japanese Americans] can't be kept locked up in concentration camps....After all, they are American citizens, and we all know that American citizens have certain privileges." Weeks later, the U.S. Supreme Court ruled that the WRA could no longer detain "concededly loyal citizens." The court's decision related specifically to Mitsuye Endo, who had filed a court case asking that she be discharged from camp and "restored to liberty." On December 18, 1944, she got her wish, although the ruling did not specifically declare the relocation of more than 110,000 Japanese and Japanese Americans unconstitutional. Only one day earlier, the WRA had announced that all camps would close within a year. On January 2, 1945, the exclusion order was finally lifted, allowing Japanese Americans to return to the West Coast.

TO UNDO A MISTAKE

Back in 1943, First Lady Eleanor Roosevelt had visited Gila River War Relocation Center to investigate charges that the WRA was "coddling" internees by not following food-rationing guidelines. In addition to observing that she did not see "any kind of extravagance," she declared: "To undo a mistake is always harder than not to create one originally, but we seldom have the foresight. Therefore we have no choice but to try to correct our past mistakes."

Although some internees protested the exclusion by pursuing court cases, resisting the draft, or responding "no" on the loyalty questionnaire, the vast majority did not want to actively protest. As many had during their years in camp, some relied on a spirit of *shikata ga nai*—"it cannot be helped"—to rebuild their lives after the war. It fell largely to their children and grandchildren, the *Sansei* and *Yonsei* who came of age during the socially and politically turbulent 1960s and 1970s, to reexamine wartime injustices and seek fulfillment of Eleanor Roosevelt's vision to correct "past mistakes."

In 1981, Michael Yoshii testified before the Commission on Wartime Relocation and Internment of Civilians (CWRIC)—established when President Jimmy Carter signed Public Law 96-317—that his family's time in camp was difficult "to discuss with my parents....Their words said one thing, while their hearts were holding something else deep inside." After listening to over 750 similar individual testimonies, the commission unequivocally concluded: "Executive Order 9066 was not justified by military necessity.... The broad historical causes that shaped these decisions were race prejudice, war hysteria, and a failure of political leadership."

The effort to correct the past mistake of the wartime relocation of Japanese Americans has been both lengthy and controversial. Locally, the effort has included annual pilgrimages to Manzanar as well as a grassroots campaign to have the site preserved. At the national level, the decades-long redress and reparations movement culminated in 1988 when President Ronald Reagan signed into law HR 422, the legislation that enabled President George H. W. Bush to begin to issue, in 1990, a letter of "sincere apology" and payment of $20,000 to each surviving internee.

Despite this official apology from the U.S. government, a lingering hurt still remains. Yet many Japanese Americans have chosen to turn this hurt into a watchful vigilance to guard against other instances of government-sanctioned racial profiling. Few have articulated this choice more eloquently than Hikoji Takeuchi, who was shot by a guard at Manzanar while taking scrap lumber to build furniture for his mother. Sixty years later, still carrying buckshot in his body, he reflected on the camp's complex legacy: "After all these days, weeks, months, years—gone under the bridge—I would like to say to the young people 'Learn how to get involved.'"

EPILOGUE

I am not a child of Manzanar, but Manzanar influenced my childhood nonetheless. Like many people, I first learned about it from the made-for-TV movie *Farewell to Manzanar,* based on the book of the same name by Jeanne Wakatsuki Houston and James D. Houston. I was nine years old at the time, watching it on a small, fuzzy black-and-white television. Even now, I can't explain why the movie—and later the book, when I read it—impacted me so profoundly. Maybe because I was the same age then as Jeanne Wakatsuki was at Manzanar. Or maybe because I'd always been interested in history and Japanese culture. Whatever it was, it made an impression on me.

I first saw Manzanar when I was thirteen and traveling Highway 395 with family friends. "That's Manzanar," our friend Marvin said nonchalantly. We stopped. I still recall standing at the abandoned sentry post, stung by blowing sand as the sun set over the Sierra Nevada. I've stood there many times since but have never been moved as I was that October evening in 1980. Like other children, I was touched by Manzanar without ever having been a child of Manzanar.

Two decades later, I arrived at Manzanar as a National Park Service employee. I'd been a park ranger for a dozen years but never thought I'd be working at Manzanar. It has been the opportunity of a lifetime to work alongside people who are such passionate and compassionate historians, designers, and educators—many of whom were Children of Manzanar—to develop the site's exhibits, audio-visual presentations, and interpretive programs.

Congress established Manzanar National Historic Site in 1992, yet preservation efforts had been going on for decades. On a cold December day in 1969, more than 150 people made a pilgrimage to Manzanar to remember and reflect. Many had been children in camp who had since grown up and now saw Manzanar differently. It was no longer just the place where they had shot marbles in front of their barracks, played baseball in the firebreaks, or danced in the mess halls. Many saw it anew as a place of silence and shame, like a dark storm over the Sierra that forever changed their lives. Ultimately, grassroots efforts, often fueled by long-buried anger and indignation, led to the recognition and preservation of Manzanar on a national level.

Today, the National Park Service preserves the tangible place to offer visitors opportunities to explore Manzanar's intangible meanings, like love and hate, loyalty and betrayal, justice and injustice, and friendship. Manzanar's main exhibit, titled *One Camp, Ten Thousand Lives; One Camp, Ten Thousand Stories*, includes many voices. Some are from Manzanar National Historic Site's ongoing oral history program, which preserves the recollections of more than 350 people. Some interviewees had never before shared their stories. Their recollections came with tears, laughter, and sometimes both. Their willingness to share their memories and photos made this book possible.

For those of us who work at Manzanar, former internees and camp staff are more than names on a roster or faces in black-and-white photos. Many are *daiji na tomodachis*—dear and treasured friends. Each year, we attend their annual "last reunion" in Las Vegas. Each year, there are fewer people, but the bonds of friendship among those who remain are deep. These Children of Manzanar, most now in their eighties, encourage and inspire our efforts to educate this and future generations.

It is mind-boggling how access to information has changed since *Farewell to Manzanar* first aired in 1976. We've gone from three television channels to three hundred. We have instant access to thousands of photos and documents online in the National Archives, the Library of Congress, and through websites dedicated to preserving and sharing Japanese American and World War II history. Images and quotes, like those in this book, are a part of all that—real stories from real people that touch our souls and remind us of our shared humanity and history.

Alisa Lynch
Manzanar, California
August 2011

Saburo Sasaki, shown above as a fourth-grader at Manzanar, shares his experiences with children and other visitors to Manzanar as a National Park Service volunteer. He chose to speak out about his wartime experiences when he witnessed Arab American coworkers experiencing racial profiling during Operation Desert Storm.

Courtesy of Manzanar National Historic Site

Left and below: Volunteer Saburo Sasaki shares his experiences with students at Manzanar, February 2007.

Photos courtesy of Manzanar National Historic Site

Manzanar High School Reunion

Our first Manzanar High School reunion was at the Ambassador Hotel in Los Angeles in 1964, in honor of our Class of '44's twentieth reunion. In 1974, we invited the Class of '43 to join us, and we held a fiftieth reunion in Las Vegas in 1994. We added the class of '45 and eventually anyone who went to school in Manzanar. A couple years later we started holding the reunion every year because we realized we were "getting old" and shouldn't wait so long to get together. Since 2004, each reunion has been billed as the "last one" but we haven't stopped yet.

To me the reunion is bonding with friends I made in camp. I never would have met some of these people had we not gone to camp. We were from different areas, but in camp we were together constantly. That's why we connected so well....At the reunions, we continue from where we left off.

—Rosie Maruki Kakuuchi, age 16 when she arrived at Manzanar

Bruce Kaji.

Joyce Nakamura.

Annie Shiraishi Sakamoto and
Celeste Loi Teodor.

Arnold Maeda.

Sam Ono.

Bo Sakaguchi.

Taira Fukushima.

George Oda.

From the 2010 Manzanar reunion, courtesy of Manzanar National Historic Site

[Manzanar High School reunions are about] lasting bonds between friends that were made in camp. We had the common experience of being yanked out of school and being put in this camp.

—Sam Ono, age 15 when he arrived at Manzanar

TERMINOLOGY

Once rooted in wartime panic and propaganda, many of the words associated with the mass removal of Japanese Americans from their West Coast homes and communities have since become outmoded. In particular, terminology used by the War Relocation Authority now appears at best euphemistic—and at worst deceptive. "I know America wants us to think that it was a relocation center," says Paul Norihiro, who arrived at Manzanar at age seventeen. "You look at the dictionary at that time. I don't see...relocation center. Concentration camp is there."

The U.S. government and military officially referred to Manzanar as a "War Relocation Center" during World War II. Regional newspapers and local residents sometimes simply called it the "Jap Camp," while President Roosevelt and many other government officials referred to it as a "concentration camp." Yet even before Manzanar shut down, "concentration camp" had assumed a far darker meaning, synonymous with Auschwitz–Birkenau and other sites of the Holocaust in Nazi Germany and Poland. Today many holocaust survivors use "death camp" to describe these sites of forced labor, incarceration, and ultimately genocide, while some former internees and others call Manzanar and the other nine centers "concentration camps."

Decades after the end of World War II, the terminology of wartime incarceration continues to elude easy consensus. Regardless of the terminology used, the fact remains that the U.S. government incarcerated more than 120,000 people of Japanese ancestry en masse without due process of law.

Keeping in mind that language, at times, fails to convey—and even masks—essential truths, the following glossary identifies commonly used terms and outlines some of the reasons why we chose to use—or not use—certain language in this book.

Assembly center: Acting in concert with the U.S. Army, the Wartime Civil Control Administration (WCCA) established seventeen temporary assembly centers following Executive Order 9066, often by hastily repurposing fairgrounds, racetracks, and other public venues. Assembly centers functioned as temporary confinement facilities, until the more permanent War Relocation Centers could be built. Manzanar originally opened as one such assembly center—the Owens Valley Reception Center—in March 1942, and became a War Relocation Center in June of that year.

Camp: Both at the time and in the years since, this term has been in widespread use as shorthand for War Relocation Centers, also commonly known during the war as "concentration camps." When some young children heard they were going to "camp," they imagined cottages and tents, not the army barracks and barbed wire they actually encountered.

Caucasian: The WRA and many of the internees routinely called the mostly all-white staff members who worked at Manzanar "Caucasian." Their residential area was sometimes called the "Caucasian housing" area, and their dining facility the "Caucasian mess hall."

Evacuee: The U.S. Army and the War Relocation Authority used the term "evacuee" to describe persons forcibly removed from their homes on the West Coast. Unless quoted from period sources, the word is not used in this book, as an "evacuee" is one who flees an impending disaster, generally voluntarily and for self-preservation; this was not the case for the Japanese Americans forcibly removed from the West Coast. In place of "evacuee," some people prefer the terms "prisoner," "inmate," or "incarceree"; others use "internee."

Exclusion Area: Authorized by Executive Order 9066 and designated by the U.S. Army, the "Exclusion Area" from which Japanese Americans were forcibly removed bisected Washington and Oregon along the Cascade mountain range and included all of California plus a section along Arizona's southern border. Following the attack on Pearl Harbor, the U.S. Army (and local, state, and federal politicians) deemed this coastal area the most strategically significant during wartime, and determined to "protect it." For a limited time following EO 9066, Japanese Americans had the option of voluntarily leaving the Exclusion Area, yet in the face of public hostility and opposition from many Western states, few exercised that option.

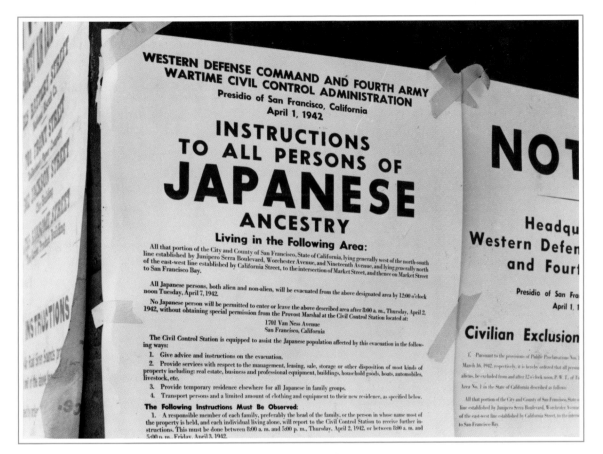

Photo by Dorothea Lange, courtesy of the National Archives and Records Administration

Executive Order 9066: Issued by President Franklin D. Roosevelt on February 19, 1942, EO 9066 authorized the Western Defense Command of the U.S. Army to demarcate the West Coast as the Exclusion Area, from which Japanese Americans and others were then removed from their homes, farms, and communities.

Internee: This term usually applies to "enemy aliens" (i.e., foreign nationals) taken captive and interned during wartime. By this definition, Japanese Americans who were U.S. citizens by birth could not be classified as "internees," whereas their *Issei* parents, who were foreign nationals, could. Thus, the only true "internees" among Japanese Americans during World War II were the several thousand *Issei* detained at Department of Justice (DOJ) camps, given individual hearings, and either moved to one of the ten War Relocation Centers or held at one of the several DOJ camps for the duration of the war. To call the entire population held in War Relocation Centers "internees" is to convey that a legal process was underway at all ten camps, which is not the case. Many now prefer the terms "inmate" and "prisoner," although "incarceree" is gaining currency as well.

Internment: In a generic context, this term refers to the *lawful* incarceration of enemy aliens. It was, however, appropriated by the WRA to describe the *unlawful* confinement of Japanese Americans during World War II. More recently, some scholars and members of the Japanese American community prefer the terms "incarceration" and "imprisonment," and these are the terms that arise in some of the first-person quotations and original source materials found in this book.

Japanese American: With nationality, cultural heritage, and citizenship status at the heart of the matter, this phrase can be unintentionally misleading. In 1942 individuals and families rounded up under EO 9066 were often simply called "the Japanese," regardless of whether they were first-generation immigrants (*Issei*) or U.S. citizens by birth (*Nisei* and *Kibei*). At the time, *Issei* could not become naturalized citizens, so "Japanese American" is typically used in this book to refer to their children, the mostly *Nisei* citizens. When speaking about both groups within Manzanar and other centers, the collective phrase "Japanese and Japanese Americans" is generally used in this book.

Loyalty questionnaire: The loyalty questionnaire is a pair of documents that the U.S. Army and WRA required be completed by all persons aged seventeen and older who were held in the camps. The questionnaire for the army was used by the U.S. Selective Service to determine eligibility for the draft, while the one for the WRA was intended to speed relocation outside the camps and to facilitate the segregation of the supposedly "disloyal" to Tule Lake Segregation Center. These questionnaires inadvertently sparked hostility toward the U.S. government and debate between family members who were suddenly called on to "forswear" all loyalty to the emperor of Japan—even if that left many *Issei* "men without a country" or offended their *Nisei* children, who had since their birth in this country held allegiance to the United States. Within weeks of the issue of the loyalty questionnaire, the WRA recognized the predicament and issued a revision eliminating the language about "forswearing."

Non-alien: In some official documents, the U.S. government called members of the American-born *Nisei* generation "non-aliens," to distinguish them from their enemy alien (or foreign national) parents. Some people believe this historic usage concealed the fact that the U.S. Army applied the Exclusion Orders to all persons of Japanese ancestry living on the West Coast, regardless of citizenship status.

Resettlement/relocation: These terms were used somewhat interchangeably by the WRA to refer to the period immediately following the Japanese Americans' release from the camps to attend college or find work in the Midwest and on the East Coast. "Resettlement" generally refers to the mandatory phase of starting over after the relocation centers closed, while "relocation" generally refers to voluntary migration outside the Exclusion Area during the war. Only rarely does "relocation" refer to the initial forced removal of Japanese Americans from the West Coast to Relocation Centers.

Segregant: The WRA used this term to refer to Japanese Americans sent to Tule Lake Segregation Center based on their responses to the loyalty questionnaire.

ACKNOWLEDGMENTS

Manzanar History Association is honored to present the stories of those whose lives were shaped so indelibly by the years they spent at Manzanar as children. Our debt to them is incalculable.

Established in 2003, Manzanar History Association (MHA) works in cooperation with the National Park Service to support educational and interpretive programs and projects at Manzanar. In the earliest days of the association, MHA Business Manager Mary Daniel envisioned a printed collection of words and images that would convey the stories of the children of Manzanar, a signature publication that would be both handsome and moving. Without her original vision, you would not be holding this book in your hands.

Special gratitude is owed as well to Mary Vocelka, whose quiet determination and unwavering commitment to the project proved both inspiring and affirming. We will hold her memory close to our hearts. We also acknowledge the efforts of Shizue Siegel, who contributed to the early development of the project. We appreciate her commitment to Japanese American history and community.

This publication was steadfastly supported by Alisa Lynch, Chief of Interpretation at Manzanar National Historic Site, whose insight and guidance were sustaining throughout. As with all of the park's projects, an equally dedicated interpretive staff provided photo research, interview transcriptions, fact-checking, and inspired feedback and review. We appreciate the efforts of the entire Manzanar staff, past and present, for preserving these stories and images and sharing them with visitors.

For generous financial support, we are indebted to the Giles W. and Elise G. Mead Foundation, to Fred and Judy Blue, and to the Friends of the Eastern California Museum. We are grateful as well to the family of photographer Toyo Miyatake for permission to use his remarkable images documenting life at Manzanar, and to all who have donated artifacts and images.

The photographs and quotations in this book came together largely through the research, both creative and meticulous, provided by Sky Hatter, lead photo researcher, and Rose Masters, lead archives researcher. Their shared devotion and unique sensibilities shaped both the tone and texture of the final product. While working with editor Heather C. Lindquist, Madison Maple contributed insightful intelligence and database skills in equal measure throughout the image selection, editing, and acquisition process. We remain enormously grateful to historian Eric L. Muller for reviewing the manuscript, although we take full responsibility for the book's final form. Naomi Hirahara and Eileen Hiraike, significant contributors to and participants in the planning process for the Manzanar Interpretive Center exhibits, both provided gentle yet candid critiques of the draft manuscript. Of course we extend heartfelt thanks to history's gracious guardians: the librarians and archivists at The Bancroft Library at the University of California, Berkeley; the Eastern California Museum, in Independence; the Japanese American National Museum, in Los Angeles; the Library of Congress, in Washington, D.C.; the Museum of History and Industry, in Seattle; the National Archives and Records Administration (NARA), in College Park, Maryland; the Japanese American Archival Collection, part of the Department of Special Collections and University Archives at California State University, Sacramento; the University of Southern California Regional History Center; and UCLA Special Collections. Michael Briggs also shared a treasured item in his personal collection—an illustrated pamphlet about the hospital school at Manzanar—and donated the original for safekeeping by the National Park Service.

The significant and continually evolving photograph, oral history, and archives collections at Manzanar National Historic Site—made possible by the generous donations from former internees, camp staff, and others—provided both the initial inspiration for this book and this rich result. With over 350 interviews conducted to date, Manzanar's oral history program has relied on the continuing diligence of dozens of Park Service interviewers, videographers, and transcribers, including Kari Coughlin, Alisa Lynch, Kirk Peterson, Richard Potashin, and Erin Brasfield Rose. As an oral history program partner, Denshō hosts digital video interviews conducted with numerous internees held at Manzanar.

And to Malcolm Margolin and Gayle Wattawa of Heyday, we are immeasurably grateful for their unwavering belief in the importance of this publication and for their remarkable editorial guidance. Although this publication's successes are shared by many, any failings are ours alone.

MANZANAR
HISTORY
ASSOCIATION

Maggie Wittenburg
Executive Director
Manzanar History Association
P.O. Box 149
Independence, CA 93526
(760) 878-2411 or (877) 424-2411
manzanar.mha@suddenlinkmail.com

REFERENCES

From the outset of this project, Manzanar History Association has hoped to share previously unseen photographs and as-yet-untold stories, many of which come from Manzanar National Historic Site. The National Park Service has been the grateful recipient of family scrapbooks and photo albums, personal belongings used in camp, and, most of all, memories. These memories survive in various forms and thanks to various sources: they have been contributed by more than 350 children of Manzanar, former WRA staff and Military Police officers, and Owens Valley residents; they have been recorded by a succession of park historians and interpretive staff; they have been stored as audio and video recordings as part of the Manzanar Oral History Program (http://www.nps.gov/manz); and in some cases they have also been disseminated digitally by Denshō, a Seattle-based nonprofit dedicated to preserving the legacy of Japanese Americans (http://www.densho.org/). Through the ID Card program (http://www.nps.gov/manz), Manzanar National Historic Site has also made a selection of these personal stories available to the public, and the site's virtual museum exhibit (http://www.nps.gov/manz) shares treasures from its archival and curatorial collection with an online audience.

While the oral history collection at Manzanar National Historic Site helps form this book's narrative spine, other significant resources comprise its heart and soul. The first among these is the remarkable collection of photographs taken by Toyo Miyatake while he was confined at Manzanar. Unlike photographers who worked on behalf of the War Relocation Authority and visited only occasionally to record life in camp, Toyo Miyatake captured candid moments in daily life and significant events in the community continuously over several years. He took his first photos in Manzanar in secret, with a wooden box camera he assembled in camp, and he later became the official camp photographer, authorized by Manzanar Project Director Ralph P. Merritt. (Initially, the U.S. govern-ment considered cameras contraband and forbade their possession by Japanese Americans, a precaution specifically waived by Merritt for Toyo Miyatake at Manzanar.) More recently, members of the Miyatake family, themselves children and grandchildren of Manzanar, have graciously shared this incomparable resource. As for the photographs taken on behalf of the WRA by Dorothea Lange, Francis Stewart, Clem Albers, Charles Mace, and others, several digital resources provide windows into this rich legacy, including the Japanese American Relocation Digital Archive, managed by The Bancroft Library at the University of California, Berkeley (http://bancroft.berkeley.edu/collections/jarda.html); the Library of Congress's Prints and Photograph Division; and the essential repository, the National Archives and Records Administration. A digital selection of "Record Group 210: Records of the War Relocation Authority, 1941–1947" may be viewed online via the National Archives' ARC search engine (http://www.archives.gov/research/arc/), and the collection in its entirety resides at the National Archives branch location in College Park, Maryland. A separate collection of photographs taken at Manzanar by Ansel Adams first appeared in his publication *Born Free and Equal* and now resides at the Library of Congress (http://memory.loc.gov/ammem/collections/anseladams/). Adams's Manzanar photos are licensed for use by the public, the photographer's gift to the American people.

A few of the voices and memories recalled in this book come from sources created during the war itself, including the camp newspaper the *Manzanar Free Press* and school newspapers (the *Campus Pepper* and the *Manzanar Whirlwind*), as well as contributions from the Associated Student Body of Manzanar High School. Anonymous interviews were conducted in camp by anthropologist Morris Opler for the Community Analysis Section of the WRA, and additional interviews were collected by "documentary historians" Togo Tanaka and Joe Masaoka. These latter sources are used only sparingly and are considered controversial by some. Yet, since they capture what are essentially eyewitness accounts of events in Manzanar as they unfolded, they are in many ways invaluable.

Several WRA publications are also cited in this book, as they provide insight into the thoughts and reactions of WRA staff and local Owens Valley residents at the time. (These include quotations from Superintendent of Education Dr. Genevieve W. Carter, Special Class teacher Eleanor Thomas, Chief Steward Joseph Winchester, and Bishop High School student Mickey Duffy.)

Most of the voices of the children of Manzanar, however, come from oral histories, interviews, public testimonies, and memoirs conducted and written decades after Manzanar shut down. The oral history collection at California State University, Fullerton—the work of former professor of public history Art Hansen as well as several others—is an essential resource. From this collection we drew upon oral histories recorded in the 1970s and 1980s and contributed by Dorothy Cragen (a school superintendent in the Owens Valley), and camp residents Sue Kunitomi Embrey, Ted Ikeda, Tamotsu Isozaki, Lillian Matsumoto, Taeko Kajiwara Nagayama, Annie Shiraishi Sakamoto, and Celeste Loi Teodor. Beginning in the 1990s, the National Park Service conducted more interviews in preparation for designing exhibits and producing media for the interpretive center, and soon expanded this work with an ongoing oral history program, whose contributors to this book include Dennis Tojo Bambauer, Rose Bannai on behalf of Shino Bannai, Joan DaValle Beyers, Sohei Hohri (Guajome Park Academy interview), Rose Honda, Mary Suzuki Ichino, Rosie Maruki Kakuuchi, Nob Kamibayashi, Frank Kikuchi, Chiyeko "Chickie" Hiraoka Matoba, Yuri Yamazaki Matsunaga, Momo Nagano, Paul Norihiro, Mas Okui (Guajome Park Academy and Harpers Ferry Center interviews), Sam Ono, Kerry Christenson Powell, Saburo Sasaki, Wilbur Sato, Dorothy Sugihara, Art Williams, and Arthur Yamada. Additionally, the Go For Broke National Education Center, which preserves the voices of Japanese American veterans of World War II, provided the quote from Bruce Kaji, and the Manzanar Committee, a grassroots organization that lobbied for the recognition of Manzanar as both a State Historic Landmark and a National Historic Site, recorded and shared the memory and legacy of Sue Kunitomi Embrey, one of its founding organizers.

No project on Manzanar is complete without referencing the testimonies gathered during 1980 as part of the gradual reparations process. These were later edited and assembled for a general audience in *Personal Justice Denied: Report of the Commission on Wartime Relocation and Internment of Civilians*. This resource helped shape the exhibits currently on display at Manzanar National Historic Site, and the script for these exhibits was, in turn, adapted to serve as the historic narrative for this book and includes excerpts from the testimonies of Grace Shinoda Nakamura and Michael Yoshii.

Other essential secondary sources include: *Years of Infamy: The Untold Story of America's Concentration Camps,* by Michi Nishiura Weglyn; *The Evacuation and Relocation of Persons of Japanese Ancestry during World War II: A Historical Study of the Manzanar War Relocation Center,* by Harlan D. Unrau; *Twice Orphaned: Voices from the Children's Village of Manzanar,* by Catherine Irwin; *Strangers from a Different Shore,* edited by Ronald Takaki; *Free to Die for Their Country: The Story of the Japanese American Draft Resisters in World War II,* by Eric L. Muller; and *Through the Eyes of Innocents: Children Witness World War II,* by Emmy E. Werner.

Excerpts from several unpublished memoirs housed at Manzanar National Historic Site also appear in these pages, specifically ones by Clara Seno Hayashi, George Atsushi Matsumoto, Raymond Muraoka, and Victor Muraoka.

HEYDAY
into California

About Heyday

Heyday is an independent, nonprofit publisher and unique cultural institution. We promote widespread awareness and celebration of California's many cultures, landscapes, and boundary-breaking ideas. Through our well-crafted books, public events, and innovative outreach programs we are building a vibrant community of readers, writers, and thinkers.

Thank You

It takes the collective effort of many to create a thriving literary culture. We are thankful to all the thoughtful people we have the privilege to engage with. Cheers to our writers, artists, editors, storytellers, designers, printers, bookstores, critics, cultural organizations, readers, and book lovers everywhere!

We are especially grateful for the generous funding we've received for our publications and programs during the past year from foundations and hundreds of individual donors. Major supporters include:

Acorn Naturalists; Alliance for California Traditional Artists; Anonymous; James J. Baechle; Bay Tree Fund; S. D. Bechtel, Jr. Foundation; Barbara Jean and Fred Berensmeier; Berkeley Civic Arts Program and Civic Arts Commission; Joan Berman; Buena Vista Rancheria; Lewis and Sheana Butler; California Civil Liberties Public Education Program, California State Library; California Council for the Humanities; The Keith Campbell Foundation; Center for California Studies; Jon Christensen; The Christensen Fund;

Compton Foundation; Lawrence Crooks; Nik Dehejia; Frances Dinkelspiel and Gary Wayne; Troy Duster; Euclid Fund at the East Bay Community Foundation; Mark and Tracy Ferron; Judith Flanders; Karyn and Geoffrey Flynn; Furthur Foundation; The Fred Gellert Family Foundation; Wallace Alexander Gerbode Foundation; Nicola W. Gordon; Wanda Lee Graves and Stephen Duscha; Alice Guild; Walter & Elise Haas Fund; Coke and James Hallowell; Hawaii Sons, Inc.; Sandra and Charles Hobson; G. Scott Hong Charitable Trust; Humboldt Area Foundation; The James Irvine Foundation; Kendeda Fund; Marty and Pamela Krasney; Kathy Kwan and Robert Eustace; Guy Lampard and Suzanne Badenhoop; LEF Foundation; Judith and Brad Lowry-Croul; Kermit Lynch Wine Merchant; Michael McCone; Michael Mitrani; Michael J. Moratto, in memory of Ernest L. Cassel; National Wildlife Federation; Steven Nightingale; Pacific Legacy, Inc.; Patagonia, Inc.; John and Frances Raeside; Redwoods Abbey; Robin Ridder; Alan Rosenus; The San Francisco Foundation; San Manuel Band of Mission Indians; Sonoma Land Trust; Martha Stanley; Roselyne Chroman Swig; Thendara Foundation; Sedge Thomson and Sylvia Brownrigg; Tides Foundation; TomKat Charitable Trust; The Roger J. and Madeleine Traynor Foundation; Marion Weber; White Pine Press; John Wiley & Sons, Inc.; The Dean Witter Foundation; Lisa Van Cleef and Mark Gunson; Bobby Winston; and Yocha Dehe Wintun Nation.

Board of Directors

Getting Involved

To learn more about our publications, events, membership club, and other ways you can participate, please visit www.heydaybooks.com.